Colgate's
Basic
Sailing
Theory

Colgate's Basic Sailing Theory

STEPHEN COLGATE

President, Offshore Sailing School Ltd.

Illustrations: John Tubb Associates

 VAN NOSTRAND REINHOLD COMPANY
New York Cincinnati Toronto London Melbourne

Jacket Photo by Walter Iooss, Courtesy of Sports Illustrated

Published by Van Nostrand Reinhold Company
135 West 50th Street, New York, N.Y. 10020

16   15

CONTENTS

FOREWORD

This book's successful use in conjunction with the Offshore Sailing School's basic course of instruction has prompted the publication of this edition, slightly augmented for beginning sailors everywhere. A few hours applied to its study will greatly speed up the learning process once you are aboard a boat. Sailing must be learned by doing, but it is twice as effectively learned by doing the *right* thing the *first* time.

I am going to throw a great deal of material at you at first. Don't be overwhelmed by it, because I realize most readers won't get it all the first time. The important terms will be repeated throughout the rest of the book, and, through repetition, the strange words and movements of this sport will soon become second nature.

Finally, a word about terminology. The "language of the sea" is traditional and comes from the days of square-rigged ships. Until you understand the strange words used in sailing, you will be unable to sail well. There are times on a boat when the action is fast, and the correct action has to be taken at the right time or disaster results. You can't afford to say, "Let that thing over there go!" when you mean, "Free the jib sheet!" Also, though I use the pronoun "he" quite often in this book, there are probably as many female sailors as male. To use "he or she" all the time is cumbersome, so whenever you read "he" remember it may just as well be "she".

Happy Sailing.

Thanks to my wife, Doris, who tirelessly typed the whole manuscript.

S.C.

TYPES OF SAILBOATS

Although we will be learning here to sail a sloop (there are more sloops around than anything else), we may just as well, at this early stage, pick up the ability to tell one type of sailing craft from another. Sailboats fall into different categories based on the number of masts they have and the location of these masts.

Single-masted sailboats are either sloops, catboats, or cutters. The sloop has two sails, a jib forward of a mainsail. A catboat has no jib and the mast is near the bow. The cutter is a sloop with the mast near the center of the boat. Actually, if the mast is more than two-fifths of the waterline length aft (behind) the point where the bow emerges from the water, it's a cutter.

Double-masted sailboats are either yawls, ketches or schooners. However, in the former two, the small mast is aft the larger. The mizzen mast, as it is called, is near the stern of the boat. A good rule of thumb is if the steering apparatus (the tiller or steering wheel) is forward of the mizzen it's a yawl,

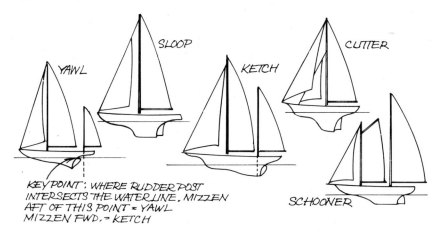

KEY POINT: WHERE RUDDER POST INTERSECTS THE WATERLINE. MIZZEN AFT OF THIS POINT = YAWL MIZZEN FWD. = KETCH

fig.1

3

and if behind the mizzen it's a ketch. There are a few instances where this guideline doesn't work. Every boat has a rudderpost that turns the rudder for steering. Where this rudderpost intersects the waterline is the real point of demarcation. If the mizzen is forward of this point, it's a ketch, if aft, it's a yawl. However, since many people don't like to steer a boat with a mast right in front of them obstructing their visibility, they have the designer arrange a steering mechanism that leads forward of the mizzen. Thus, the wheel is forward of the mizzen, the rudderpost is aft, and it's still a ketch.

If the boat has two masts and the forward mast or "foremast" is smaller or the same size as the after mast, it's a schooner. Schooners can have three, four or even more masts. None of the masts on a schooner is called the mizzen. Well, *almost* never! The largest schooner ever built was the Thomas F. Lawson, launched in 1902, with seven masts. Beginning at the bow, its masts were called the Foremast, Main, Mizzen, Frigger, Jigger, Driver and Spanker. But you'll never need to know that, so try to forget it . . .

DIMENSIONS AND PARTS
OF THE BOAT

Open any boating publication to the design section and you will find a list of dimensions for the particular design being commented upon. These are usually abbreviated.

LOA stands for "length overall." This is the total length of the boat from the bow to the stern in a straight line, not including any bowsprit.

The "load waterline" or simply "waterline length" is abbreviated as LWL. This is the straight-line distance from the point where the bow emerges from the water to the point where the stern emerges from the water.

As you can see in Figure 2, the topsides of the boat are the sides extending from the waterline up to the deck. If you hear someone say, "Look at the beautiful bright topsides on that boat," it's not just a comment on the vessel's intelligence. He means the boat has natural wood topsides that have been varnished. "Brightwork" is varnished wood trim. Another person in the cabin of a cruising boat may say, "I'm going topsides." This has nothing to do with the topsides of the boat, it means he's going up on deck, another non-sequitur of the sailing idiom.

The next common dimension of a boat is its draft (DRA). This is the distance from the water level to the deepest part of the boat. If a boat sailing along touches bottom in three feet of water, then her draft is three feet or she "draws" three feet, which is another way of saying the same thing. Centerboard sailboat designs will usually state two drafts for the boat, such as, "She draws six inches with the board up and four feet with the board down." It is obviously important to know how much your boat draws so you can look at the depth of water on a chart and avoid areas that are shallower than your draft.

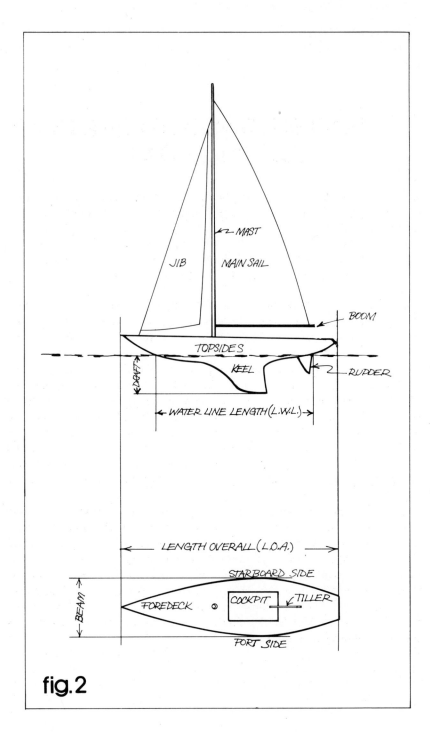

fig.2

Common advertisements in boating magazines can be incomprehensible at first, yet how could you buy a boat if you didn't know what the ads or the dealers were saying? Here is a typical ad from YACHTING magazine.

"She has a minimal wetted surface hull, high aspect ratio keel, large separation between the CLR and rudder, and a high ballast/displacement ratio. Her trimtab is linked to separate rudder for reduced leeway and better control, and she has high aspect ratio rig with large foretriangle. The PT-40 is light enough to surf readily, yet heavy enough to carry her sail."

In short, you should understand such descriptions.

The beam of the boat (BM) is its maximum width, not its width at deck level as one might expect. Figure 3 (Ballast Displacement Ratio) shows the cross-section of a keelboat where the maximum width is about in the middle of the "topsides" (sides of the boat), so it's at that point where the beam is measured. When the topsides curve inward to meet the deck, rather than go straight up, the result is called "tumblehome." It's a weight saving device in classes of sailboats that specify a minimum beam in their rules, but allow wide design latitude otherwise.

Another term bandied about by manufacturers, salesmen and sailors is "aspect ratio" (Figure 4). Notice it was used twice in the YACHTING ad quoted, in regard to the keel and then to the rig or sails. It is the relationship of the height of anything to its breadth. If a sail is 60 feet measured along the mast and 15 feet along the boom, then the aspect ratio is stated as 8 to 1, or AR = 8. One might think this should be 4 to 1 (60 feet divided by 15 feet) and is often stated in such terms, but that would be the AR of a rectangle which has twice the average width of a triangle with the same base. So we double it and arrive at an AR of 8:1. If the same boat added five feet to her boom, she would have a lower aspect ratio -- 60 feet divided by 20 feet = 3, and this doubled equals an AR of 6 to 1. The importance of aspect ratio has to do with boat performance. A high aspect ratio sail goes better upwind whereas a low AR sail works better with the wind pushing from behind.

Another ratio stated often is the ballast-displacement ratio of a boat. This is the relationship of weight of the iron or lead "ballast" in the keel (used like a pendulum to keep the boat upright) to the total weight of the boat. For instance, if a 10,000 pound boat has 4000 pounds of lead in its keel for ballast, it has a 40% ballast-displacement ratio. The higher the ratio, the more stability the boat has. A ratio of about 50% is very good for a cruising boat.

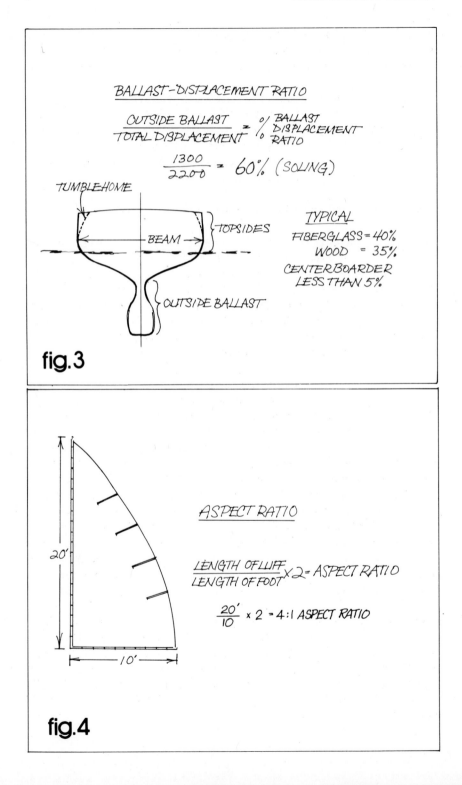

BALLAST-DISPLACEMENT RATIO

$$\frac{OUTSIDE\ BALLAST}{TOTAL\ DISPLACEMENT} = \%\ \begin{array}{l}BALLAST\\ DISPLACEMENT\\ RATIO\end{array}$$

$$\frac{1300}{2200} = 60\% \ (SOLING)$$

TUMBLEHOME

TOPSIDES

BEAM

OUTSIDE BALLAST

TYPICAL
FIBERGLASS = 40%
WOOD = 35%
CENTERBOARDER
LESS THAN 5%

fig.3

ASPECT RATIO

$$\frac{LENGTH\ OF\ LUFF}{LENGTH\ OF\ FOOT} \times 2 = ASPECT\ RATIO$$

$$\frac{20'}{10} \times 2 = 4:1\ ASPECT\ RATIO$$

20'

10'

fig.4

RIGGING AND SAILS

Now that we are able to look at a sailboat and characterize its type, the next step is to know the names of the various items of rigging and sails.

Rigging

Rigging, all the wire and line (rope) used aboard a sailboat, is broken down into two major categories -- running rigging and standing rigging.

Running rigging consists of all the lines on a boat that are easily adjusted. "Halyards" raise and lower the sails, and "sheets" adjust them in and out laterally. Halyards and sheets are the major components of running rigging and take the name of the sail to which they are attached. A main halyard

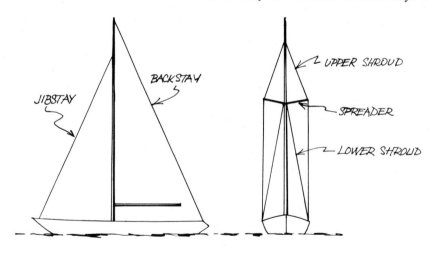

fig.5

9

raises and lowers the mainsail. A jibsheet adjusts the trim of the jib. At this juncture, let's clear up another possible source of confusion. The "trim" of the jib or of any sail is the angle of that sail to the wind direction at a given point in time. But to "trim" a jib is to pull it in with the jib sheet, and to "ease" or "start" it, is to let it out.

Standing rigging consists of the wires that hold up the masts of a sailboat. It too is broken down into two major categories -- "stays" and "shrouds." The stays keep the mast from falling "fore and aft" (over the bow or the stern). The shrouds keep it from falling "athwartships" (over the side of the boat.

The standing "backstay" is found on most boats and runs from the head (top) of the mast back to the deck at the middle of the stern. The stay leading forward is called the "headstay" if it leads from the head of the mast to the bow, the "jibstay" if it leads from partway down the mast to the bow, or the "forestay" if it leads to the middle of the foredeck which is the area of deck forward to the foremost mast. Many sailors use these three terms for stays interchangeably, however, so don't get too confused by them.

Because shrouds lead from the edges of the deck up to attachment points on the mast, the angle they make to the mast is more acute than that of the stays. For this reason, the shrouds that lead highest on the mast -- the "upper shrouds" -- run through the end of metal or wooden struts or tubes on either side of the mast. These tubes are called "spreaders" since they spread the angle the shroud makes with the mast. This results in better support for the upper section of the mast. It also results in compression load on the spreaders which tends to bend the mast at that point. To counteract this bend, most boats have another set of shrouds -- the "lower shrouds" -- on either side of the mast leading from the base of the spreaders to the edge of the deck. Since these originate lower down the mast; the angle they make with the mast is wide enough to eliminate the need for extra spreaders, as you can see from Figure 5.

Sails

Modern mainsails, pronounced "mains'ls", but more often called "mains," and jibs are made of Dacron, a Dupont product, in the United States. The important property of Dacron is that it stretches less than most synthetics on the market. A sailmaker cuts and sews a sail in a desirable shape. He doesn't want it to lose this shape under the pressure of the wind, so his aim in choosing cloth is to have as little stretch as possible, or at least a predictable amount.

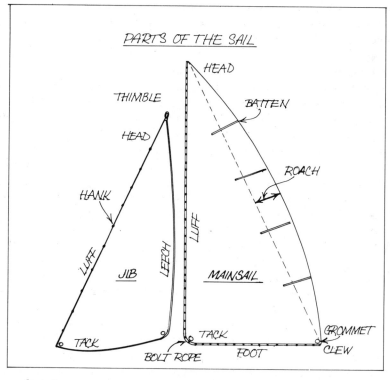

fig. 6

When completed, the sail is triangular in shape. The three edges of the sail are the "luff" -- the leading edge, the "leech" -- the trailing edge, and the "foot" -- the bottom edge. The three corners are the "head" at the top, the "tack" -- the forward lower corner, and the "clew" -- the after lower corner. Notice in Figure 6 that a straight dotted line between the head and the clew indicates that the sail is convex. The material outside this line is called "roach." If the sail were concave, as many jibs are, it wouldn't have any roach. It would still have a leech, though, since that is just the area of the sail between the head and the clew.

The foot and luff of the mainsail are reinforced by a rope called the "boltrope." This is the only rope on a boat which we do not refer to as line. The sailcloth is sewn to it, as are the sail slides that go on the sail-track on the mast of larger boats. On small boats the boltrope goes inside a groove in the mast and boom, taking the place of sail slides.

The boltrope reinforces the luff and foot, but something is needed to keep the leech of the sail from unraveling. The sailmaker sews a strip of doubled over material along the edge which is called "tabling." Sometimes he incorporates in the tabling a light line that is attached at the head and is adjustable at the clew. This is called a "leech cord" or "pucker string" and is used to reduce leech flutter which occasionally occurs along the trailing edge of the sail. Also along the leech, evenly spaced, are pockets that hold strips of wood or plastic called "battens." The purpose of the battens is to support the roach of the sail, which would otherwise flop over by gravity. A typical batten for a 25 foot boat might be 1 inch wide, 24 inches long and taper from about 1/4 inch thick to 1/8 inch thick over its length. The thin end enters the batten pocket first because it's more flexible and will have to follow the curve of the sail. There is sometimes a hole in the thick end, a carry over from the time when battens were tied in the pockets. Now the opening is from above and tying is no longer necessary.

Sails are the driving force of a sailboat and just as any engine needs care, so do sails. Sunlight deteriorates Dacron so, at least when not in use, they should be kept out of it. Dried salt from spray makes them heavy as the salt picks up moisture from the air each time out and dirt particles tend to shorten the life of the material. So sails should be washed occasionally with warm water and mild soap.

Sails should be folded before placing them in the sailbag. They have been treated with a filler to reduce porosity and stretch. Stuffing them in the sail-bag breaks down the filler in the cloth and reduces its life. The sails come out of the sailbag completely wrinkled and it may take an hour or so of sailing to smooth the wrinkles out. Also, wrinkles reduce sail area. Try this experiment: Lay a piece of typewriter paper on a table and crumple up a second piece. Now, smooth out the crumpled piece and lay it down on top of the first piece, lining up the top edges. You'll probably end up about 1/16 inch short at the bottom and this is over a span on only 11 inches! Furthermore, wrinkles tend to disrupt the airflow over the sail. There's not much sense for sailmakers to do research for smoother, tighter weave cloths if the sailor messes it up with a bunch of wrinkles.

So get in the habit of folding the sails of any small boat after each sail. This obviously can't be done with the sails of large cruising boats, but the forces are larger and the wrinkles tend to "sail out" quickly anyway, so there is little need. The proper way is described in Appendix IV. Remember to make the final roll such that the clew is on the outside in the case of a mainsail and the tack is outside in the case of a jib, since these are the corners you need first respectively when putting on, or "bending on," the sails.

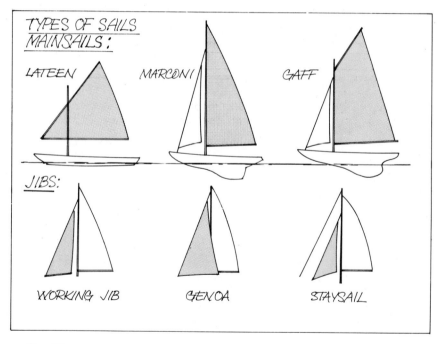

fig.7

GETTING UNDERWAY

Whether you buy or charter, rent or borrow your sailboat, it will either be tied to a float, kept out on a mooring or "drysailed" (launching it by trailer or by hoist each time you want to sail it.) The latter is much more work, but has advantages for the racing sailor. First, the bottom won't get fouled -- slime and seaweed won't have a chance to grow on it. This is more crucial in salt water than in fresh, but will definitely slow the boat down in either case. Second, the boat won't have a chance to absorb water, thereby making it heavier and slower. Even fiberglass boats are "hydroscopic" in that they absorb water. The other reasons for drysailing a boat are if mooring or docking facilities are unprotected, inadequate or unavailable.

Getting to a Moored Boat

Since most sailboats are kept at moorings, we'll direct our attention to these. When you load your dinghy to row or motor out to the moored sailboat, always step into the middle of the boat and not on the seats. The lower you get the weight in the boat, the more stable it will be, so sit down immediately before someone else attempts to step into the boat. Load the middle of the boat first in order to keep the trim level. The "fore and aft trim" of any boat is the relationship of its design waterline, which is painted on the boat, to the surface of the water. You might say a sailboat was "down by the bow" if it had too much weight (crew or equipment) forward or "dragging the stern" if it had too much weight aft. So keep the dingly level or slightly down by the stern and don't overload it.

Whoever is rowing, or running the outboard may ask you, once you are seated, to "trim the boat." This means you should ease your seat (and weight) to port or starboard so that the dinghy rides level, making it easier to row, and safer in choppy water.

"Freeboard" is the distance from the edge of the deck to the water when the boat is level. If the boat is so heavily loaded that it sinks down in the water leaving only about six inches of freeboard, any rolling by waves or shifting of passenger weight may cause the dinghy to "ship" water over the side (fill up). Before long it will sink as the weight of the water lowers the freeboard even more.

Boarding Your Boat

If your moored sailboat is a small (under 20 feet long) centerboard type, when you reach it you should step in the middle of the cockpit *and* lower the centerboard for stability.

The centerboard is a metal or wood plate that is pinned at the forward end and pivots down in an arc when lowered, as opposed to a "daggerboard" that doesn't pivot but raises or lowers vertically. The housing for the centerboard is called the "centerboard trunk." The board is usually kept in the "up" position when the boat is moored, so seaweed won't have a chance to form on it.

Since most centerboards are relatively light weight, they don't act much like a keel (a heavy fixed weight well below the surface of the water). When it is lowered, stability is improved, but crew weight on one side of the boat or the other has the most effect. Lowering the centerboard, however, slows up the rolling motion of the boat, so if you step to one side the boat won't tip so fast and you can get your balance back before the boat capsizes (turns over).

The reason for stepping into the cockpit rather than forward on the deck is again one of stability. Most planing sailboats (those that can skim the surface of the water at high speeds, much like skipping a stone) are veed in the bow and have a reasonably flat run aft. If you step in the bow you push the veed part deeper and raise the flat stable part out of the water, so the boat *has* to tip.

Getting aboard a keelboat is easier in that you don't have to be concerned with capsizing it. The launch or dinghy is usually being held next to the sailboat by an operator near the stern and a common error is for someone near the bow of the launch to get out first and let the bow drift off. Either the person in the bow of the launch should be the last off and should hold it in close for the others, or he should get onto the sailboat and hold the bow of the launch in with the "painter" (the launch's bow line).

When getting aboard make sure you don't pinch your fingers between the launch and the sailboat. If the sailboat is high-sided and there are no lifelines to grab, the safest way to board, particularly if it's rough, is to turn around, sit on the deck and then swing your legs aboard.

Setting Sail

In most types of boats the process of setting sail is fairly much the same. For the parts of the sail following, refer to Figure 6. Locate the clew of the "main" and run the foot out along the boom. The boom will either have a groove that the foot runs inside or a track which accommodates slides sewn on the foot of the sail. One person will have to feed the slides onto the track or the foot into the groove, while another pulls the clew out to the end of the boom. A pin is placed through the tack corner, the "outhaul" attached to the clew and the foot may then be stretched out tight and "secured" or cleated.

The battens are placed in the batten pockets, with the thin end entering first. Check that you have the right length in the proper pocket. Starting at the tack, follow along the luff to make sure there are no twists in the sail. Attach the main halyard, looking "aloft" (up) in case it's "fouled" (twisted) around a spreader or backstay. If the main luff has slides, put them all on the mast track starting at the head of the sail. If the mast is grooved, you will have to feed the luff of the sail in the groove as it goes up, but first get the jib ready.

The tack of the jib is the corner that is attached first. There are a number of ways to quickly identify this corner: (1) the sailmaker's label or emblem is almost always located there since there is an International Yacht Racing Union rule to this effect, (2) the angle at the tack is much wider than the angle at the head, (3) the jib hanks or snaps usually attach to the jibstay from right to left for right-handed people -- in other words, the opening in the snap is on the left. If you dump a large sail out of the bag, just by looking at one jib hank you can tell which way to follow the luff to the tack. (4) A good crew, knowing that the tack is needed first, will leave that corner on top of the sail after "bagging it" (putting it away in a sailbag). And (5) on larger boats, "TACK" is often written at the corner so there can be no mistake.

Next attach the tack and start hanking on the snaps from bottom up. If you start at the top of the sail you would have to hold the sail up and hank on each snap underneath. This would get mighty heavy after awhile. Also, the sail would be up high where a gust of wind could blow it overboard. So you start with the tack first and pull the sail forward between your legs to keep it low, protected from the wind, and to avoid draping it over the side of the bow in the water.

The jib sheets (the lines that pull the jib in and out) are now attached and led through their proper "leads" (blocks, or pulleys, that adjust the trim angle of the jib) and either a "figure-eight" knot or "stop" knot as shown in Figures 8 and 9 is made in the end of each sheet. This keeps the end of the line from running out of the jib lead when you let it go. Of the two knots, the "stop" knot is probably the more sure. Now attach the jib halyard that will pull the sail up and you're all set to go.

FIGURE EIGHT KNOT

1.   2.   3.

fig.8

STOP KNOT

1.   2.

3.   4.

fig.9

The mainsail is the first sail to raise for various reasons. It acts like a weather vane and keeps the boat headed into the wind. This is most important on a cruising boat since you are apt to motor out of a harbor, head the boat into the wind and idle the engine while the mainsail is raised. If the boat swings broadside to the wind, which might happen if you raise the jib first, the mainsail will fill with wind, press against the rigging, and bind on the sail track making it virtually impossible to raise the sail further.

The same problems arise on smaller boats, but if you start from a mooring, the boat automatically "lays" with her bow pointed directly into the wind, unless the current is strong enough to overpower the wind's effect on the boat, in which case the wind can't be strong enough to give problems in sail raising. With small boats sailing from moorings, therefore, the only reason to raise the jib last is because the jib flails around during and after raising. This tangles the jib sheets and causes an awful commotion on a windy day, which continues until the main is raised and you are underway. The flailing also reduces the life of the jib, because it breaks down the cloth fibers and fatigues the sail at the batten pockets.

ONE IMPORTANT ITEM TO REMEMBER WHEN RAISING SAILS IS THAT ALL THE SHEETS MUST BE COMPLETELY LOOSE so the sail will line up with the wind rather than fill. At the same time, all lines that might be holding the boom down, like the downhaul and boom vang, must be eased so that nothing can keep the main from going all the way up. A crew member should hold the after end of the boom up in the air to relieve the pull of the leech of the sail.

Leaving the Mooring

Before leaving the mooring, let's get a couple of basic terms clear: *starboard* and *port* are two terms in as constant use aboard a boat as *fore* and *aft.* Starboard is right and port is left. Some remember this by the fact that "port" and "left" have the same number of letters. It's been said that the words came from sailing ships of long ago that used a sweep or oar for steering. It was called the "steering board" and was over the right side of the boat when one faced the bow. Thus the right side was called the "steering board" side and later, the starboard side. The left side was clear to lay next to a dock while the boat was in port and became the "port" side.

Now we're ready to sail away, but since the boat is headed directly into the wind at a mooring and is not moving through the water, it is what we call "in irons" or "in stays." This can happen at other times when a boat attempts to change tacks by turning into the wind, is stopped by a wave, and loses "steerageway" or "headway." In order to steer a boat, water must be flowing past the rudder. If the boat is "dead in the water" (motionless) the rudder is useless, so the sails have to be used in its place.

The sails, because the boat is pointing directly into the wind, are "luffing" (shaking). To "fill" the sails, you will have to place the boat at an angle to the wind. Usually this angle is 45° or more and when the boat reaches this position the sails will fill with wind and the boat will start moving forward. Until that point, the sails have to be manually forced out against the wind to fill them. This is called "backing" the sail. If you want to turn the bow of the boat to starboard (to the right) you hold the jib out to port as in Figure 10A. The wind hits the port side of the jib and pushes the bow to starboard. After the boat is pushed 45° to the wind, the jib is released and trimmed normally on the starboard side.

Though backing the jib is the fastest and surest method of falling off onto the desired tack, there are other ways. If the boat is drifting backwards as in Figure 10B, put the tiller to starboard. The rudder will turn the stern of the boat in the direction of the arrow and the boat will "fall off" onto the port tack.

You might be sailing a small boat that has no jib. In that case you can push the main out against the wind. This starts the boat moving backwards and turns the stern to the opposite to the side that you are holding the main. In other words, if you back the main to the starboard side, the stern will go to port as in Figure 10C. Help the boat turn by putting the tiller to starboard as described above.

If you are sailing a yawl or a ketch you can back the mizzen out against the wind in the same manner and with the same effect as backing the main of a small boat. Note Figure 10D.

The standard procedure when leaving a mooring is for a crew member to untie the mooring line, but hold onto the end of it (or, if possible, pull the boat forward with it to gain a little forward momentum) while he backs the jib. When the bow is definitely swinging in the desired direction he releases the mooring line and is off sailing!

As the boat starts moving forward, the rudder becomes effective. Though it eventually becomes automatic, at first one has to think which way to push the tiller to steer a sailboat. As the boat sails along, water flows past the rudder. When the rudder is turned it deflects the water flow and pushes the stern opposite from the direction of the deflected flow.

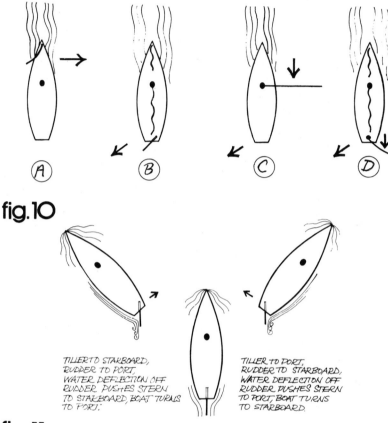

fig.10

TILLER TO STARBOARD,
RUDDER TO PORT,
WATER DEFLECTION OFF
RUDDER PUSHES STERN
TO STARBOARD, BOAT TURNS
TO PORT.

TILLER TO PORT,
RUDDER TO STARBOARD,
WATER DEFLECTION OFF
RUDDER PUSHES STERN
TO PORT, BOAT TURNS
TO STARBOARD.

fig.11

Study Figure 11. The hull and keel of the boat act as a pivotal point, so the bow goes opposite the stern. When leaving a float in a cruising boat under power, one often sees the new owner try to swing the bow out too sharply. The stern bumps along the pilings because the skipper is so intent on turning the bow he forgets he is actually throwing the stern towards the dock. To turn to port he has to push the tiller to starboard and vice-versa which confuses many beginners. It's interesting to note that the fireman who steers the rear wheels of a hook and ladder truck is called the "tillerman". The theory is the same. There's no easy way to remember how to steer a sailboat, practice is the key. Just sail on a "beam reach" (see Figures 12 and 13) and make a series of small turns to get the feel of it.

POINTS OF SAILING

Finding the Direction of the Wind

Sailing is much like riding a bicycle. When you finally catch on, you never lose the knack. Just as balance is the most important skill in bicycling, feeling the relationship of the wind to the sails is the key to sailing. Since it is impossible to actually see the wind, it usually takes quite a while for the beginner to reliably figure out where it's coming from, especially in "light air." When asked to point towards the wind a novice often points as much as 90° away from the true wind direction. And even should he point it out fairly well the first time, after he has turned the boat in a different direction the novice often isn't aware of the relative wind direction change since he's still facing the bow of the boat. Thus, if he pointed 50° off the bow the first time, he's apt to point in the same direction the second time even though the boat has changed heading.

The difficulty arises from the fact that all diagrams describing "points of sailing" (as those that follow) show the wind as nice clear black lines. The points of sailing describe the boat when sailing at various angles to the wind direction. The novice who understands fully well from books or the classroom just what is a "beat," a "reach" or a "run" is sometimes hard-pressed out on the water to relate the boat's heading to the wind direction, because the wind is not visible as in diagrams.

The way we solve this little enigma for the novice is to have him point at the wind before any maneuver, at least the first time out. We won't let him make any move until he spots the wind correctly. The easiest source of this information are "telltales," pieces of wool tied to the shrouds, which indicate wind direction.

A note here for the racing skipper: "Angora" wool is the lightest and most sensitive, and red is the most visible. Strips of ribbon or nylon stockings are not anywhere near as sensitive and feathers are next to useless.

23

Another source is the "masthead fly" -- a swiveling weather vane at the top
of the mast. This should be extremely light for three reasons. The first is
the undesirability of weight near the top of the mast which causes heeling
and pitching. The second is to make it sensitive to very light breezes. And
the third is to reduce the moment of inertia of the masthead fly. In other
words, you want it to turn to the new wind direction and settle down
quickly rather than swing past it due to inertia. There are other indications
of wind direction, but if the beginner sticks to telltales and the masthead
fly, he can't go wrong.

In describing the direction of the wind with respect to the sails, we refer to
a "tack." A boat is *always* "on a tack" unless in the process of changing
tacks. Most people remember that if the wind is coming over the port side
of the boat, she is on the port tack. This is fine until the boat is sailing
directly downwind and the wind is coming over the stern. What tack is it
on then? If you remember that legally a boat is on the tack corresponding
to the opposite side her main boom is on, you can't go wrong. If the
mainsail is on the starboard side of the boat, the boat is on the port tack
and vice-versa. When the boat is "closehauled" (Figures 12 and 16), however,
the boom is near the middle of the boat and it may be difficult for the
beginner to determine which side it's on. Imagine which side it will be on if
eased.

If the above methods are still confusing, there is a third way of determining tacks. If the wind is filling the port side of the mainsail, the boat is
on a port tack.

Don't be confused by the three different uses of the word "tack." First,
the forward lower corner of a sail is called the tack. Second, as mentioned
before, a sailboat is always on the starboard or port tack, depending which
side the wind is blowing. And third, a boat that is changing from one tack
to the other is "tacking." There's a simple, logical reason for this apparent
confusion. In the days of square-rigged ships, the forward lower corner of
the squaresail on the windward side was called the tack. If the wind was
coming over the port side of the ship, the port half of the squaresail was
farthest forward, so the port lower corner became the tack, and the ship
was on the port tack. When the ship changed course so the wind came over
the starboard side, the squaresails were pivoted around so the starboard
half of the sail was forward and the lower starboard corner became the
tack, thus the ship has changed tacks or tacked and was now on the
starboard tack.

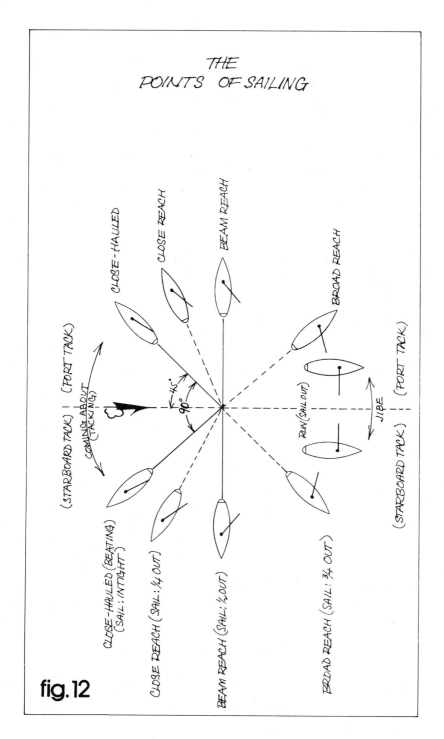

THE POINTS OF SAILING

fig. 12

Reaching

The first and easiest point of sailing for the novice to practice is the "beam reach."

If he points at the wind and then turns the boat so that the wind is coming over the side of the boat at right angles to the pointing, he is sailing on a beam reach as in the diagram. This is a pleasant and forgiving point of sailing in that the boat doesn't heel (lean over) excessively and the helmsman can wander off course without accidently tacking or jibing. So a beam reach is a good heading for the beginner to get used to steering a boat.

After a little practice at steering, settle down on the beam reach with the wool telltales streaming right across the boat. Point your arm at the wind and turn the boat slightly towards the direction you're pointing. You are now sailing on a "close reach," in other words, closer to the wind than before. Your sails will start to flutter (luff), so you will have to pull them in to keep them full of wind. Picture the sail like a flag waving in the breeze. If you grab the tail of the flag and pull it towards the wind (crosswind) it will fill with air and stop flapping. This is like trimming (pulling in) the sail. As you let the flag go slowly (like easing a sail) it will start to flutter where it lines up with the wind. So, as you sail along on a reach, the test to determine whether your sail is trimmed properly is to ease it until it starts to luff at the leading edge, (miraculously) called the "luff" of of the sail and then trim it back in a little until the luff stops.

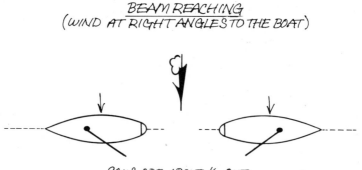

BEAM REACHING
(WIND AT RIGHT ANGLES TO THE BOAT)

SAILS ARE ABOUT ½ OUT

fig. 13

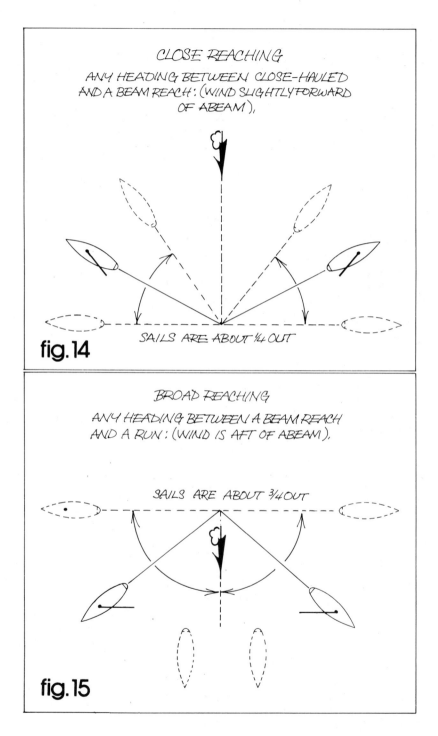

CLOSE REACHING

ANY HEADING BETWEEN CLOSE-HAULED
AND A BEAM REACH: (WIND SLIGHTLY FORWARD
OF ABEAM).

SAILS ARE ABOUT ¼ OUT

fig. 14

BROAD REACHING

ANY HEADING BETWEEN A BEAM REACH
AND A RUN: (WIND IS AFT OF ABEAM).

SAILS ARE ABOUT ¾ OUT

fig. 15

Sailing Closehauled

If you continue turning the boat in the direction you are pointing your arm, you will have to continue trimming in the sails to keep them from luffing. There will come a time when you can't trim in the sails any tighter, because they're almost in the middle of the boat. At this point you are sailing "closehauled" or as close to the wind as possible without actually luffing.

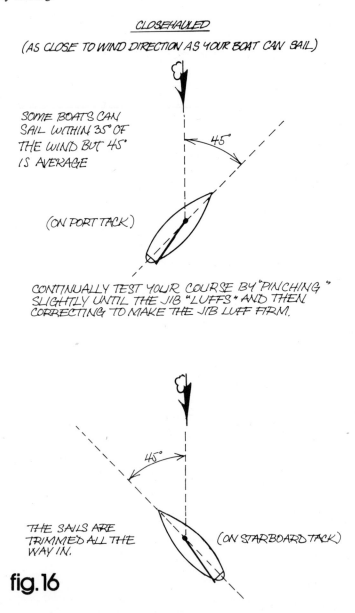

CLOSEHAULED

(AS CLOSE TO WIND DIRECTION AS YOUR BOAT CAN SAIL)

SOME BOATS CAN SAIL WITHIN 35° OF THE WIND BUT 45° IS AVERAGE

45°

(ON PORT TACK)

CONTINUALLY TEST YOUR COURSE BY "PINCHING" SLIGHTLY UNTIL THE JIB "LUFFS" AND THEN CORRECTING TO MAKE THE JIB LUFF FIRM.

45°

THE SAILS ARE TRIMMED ALL THE WAY IN.

(ON STARBOARD TACK)

fig. 16

Since the sails are trimmed as tight as possible the crew can do nothing about it if the sails start luffing. The helmsman has to head more away from the wind to get the sails full again if this happens. When closehauled, it is up to the helmsman to keep the sails full. When on a reach the responsibility transfers to the crew to keep the sails full by adjusting them in or out while the helmsman steers a straight course.

Any change of course away from the wind is called "heading down" or "falling off" and any change towards the wind is "coming up" or "hardening up."

Sailors use many terms, but those that have the connotation of up or high imply being too close to the wind. Down or low imply being too far from the wind or more broadside to it. If someone says, "You're too high," he means that you are too close to the wind and your sails are either luffing slightly or about to.

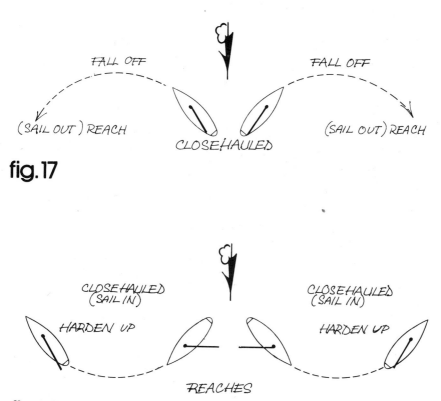

fig. 17

fig. 18

When sailing closehauled most boats head within 45 degrees of the wind, though some can "point" even higher (sail closer to the wind). One question often asked is how can one know the exact number of degrees your boat will sail relative to the wind. The compass gives the answer. Sail on the port tack closehauled as close to the wind as possible without luffing and record your heading. Let's say it's due north. Now sail the starboard tack closehauled and again look at your compass. The difference will likely be about 90 degrees, the compass will read due west. We assume that the wind splits right down the middle of the two tacks. Dividing the number of degrees (90°) in half, we assume you are sailing 45 degrees from the wind when closehauled. If the two headings were 80 degrees apart, it means your boat is able to sail within 40 degrees of the wind. Some boats can sail as close as 30 to 35 degrees to the wind, but this is very unusual. For our purposes we will use 45 degrees as a rule of thumb.

Running

We've covered two points of sailing -- closehauled and a reach. The third is a "run" or "running free" and is essentially sailing with the wind pushing the boat from behind. Notice in Figure 12 that the closehauled and reaching sails are at much the same angle to the wind no matter what point of sailing. As we fall off to a run, we ease the sails out to maintain this angle. We reach a point, however, seen in Figure 19, when we can't ease the sail out any further because the boom has reached the shrouds that hold up the mast. We may want to turn further, so the solution is to bring the boom over to the other side of the boat.

Whenever the boom crosses the centerline of the boat (an imaginary line from the bow to the middle of the stern) you have changed tacks. Any change of tacks (from port tack to starboard tack or vice-versa) downwind -- with the bow turning away from the source of the wind and the wind coming over the stern -- is called a "jibe." Remember the necessary ingredient is *changing tacks*. Just changing course downwind is not jibing. Until the boom crosses the centerline, you are just "falling off."

There are two commands when jibing. When the skipper issues the command, "Prepare to jibe!" the crew's job is to start trimming (pulling in) the mainsheet, so the boom won't have so far to travel when it starts swinging across.

Once the wind starts to fill the other side of the mainsail, the boom swings across the boat with fury and woe to the head that gets in its path. By trimming it in first, the crew keeps the swing of the boom to a minimum. When the helmsman sees that the boom is near the middle of the boat he gives the command of execution, "Jibe Ho!" and turns the boat. As soon as the boom crosses the centerline of the boat, the crew eases it out quickly on the other side to keep the boat from heeling excessively. This process varies with different types of boats. Many throw the boom over to the other side rather than trimming in, but this is not a safe way for the beginner to jibe until he knows his capabilities and more about the boat.

Beginners often get the boat on a run with the boom way out over the side of the boat and, after saying "Jibe Ho!" turn the boat the wrong way. If you just remember to turn the bow of the boat towards the same side of the boat as the boom, you won't make that mistake.

Because of the distance the boom has to travel across the boat when jibing, a major concern is an accidental jibe when the boom comes swinging across unexpectedly. This can happen when the wind comes over the same side of the boat as the main boom. Consider the following diagrams.

RUNNING
(BEFORE -THE- WIND)

SAILS ARE
SLACKED
ALL THE
WAY OUT,

PORT TACK   STARBOARD TACK

fig.19

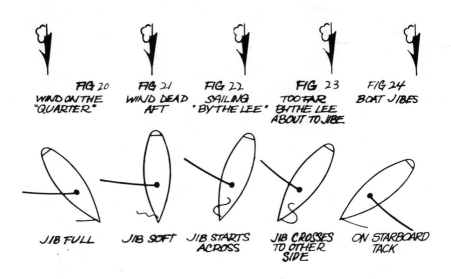

FIG 20
WIND ON THE
"QUARTER"

FIG 21
WIND DEAD
AFT

FIG 22
SAILING
"BY THE LEE"

FIG 23
TOO FAR
BY THE LEE
ABOUT TO JIBE

FIG 24
BOAT JIBES

JIB FULL

JIB SOFT

JIB STARTS
ACROSS

JIB CROSSES
TO OTHER
SIDE

ON STARBOARD
TACK

In Figure 20 the wind is opposite the boom, thus no fear of an accidental jibe. The jib is full.

In Figure 21 the boat is sailing dead (directly) downwind and is in no danger of jibing unless the helmsman is sloppy in his steering or a wave throws the stern to one side. The jib is being blanketed by the main (no wind is getting to it).

Figure 22 shows the wind on the same side as the boom. Though dangerous, a boat can sail along like this. It's called sailing "by-the-lee." The wind is coming over the "leeward" side of the boat. You might think this would make it the windward side because the wind is now hitting that side first, but right of way rules, to avoid confusion, define the "leeward side" as the side over which the main boom is carried.

If you sail too far by-the-lee as in Figure 23, the wind will catch the other side of the sail and throw it across the boat. The boom will raise up in the air, unless held down by a "boom vang," and can catch on the backstay if the latter is close to the end of the boom as in some boats. The accidental jibe is often called a "flying jibe" and if the boom catches on the backstay, it's called a "goosewing." The first warning of an accidental jibe is the jib coming across the boat. When the jib crosses to the other side, the main won't be far behind so WATCH OUT!

One of my favorite friends is a grand lady who sails Atlantic Class sailboats which are 30-foot sloops of identical design. She is over 80 years old and still racing, almost always with an all-girl crew and often with someone who has never sailed before. She told me the following incident happened when she was in her 70's. One of her crew had never sailed before, and so was assigned the job of trimming in the mainsail for the jibe around a mark while the rest of her crew, who were more experienced, took care of more difficult tasks.

Beforehand the skipper carefully described the job: "Trim the mainsail with the mainsheet, but don't make it fast." In other words, pull in the line that adjusts the sail in and out but don't cleat or secure it. Just before the mark she gave the command, "Prepare to jibe!" at which time the new crew member started pulling in the mainsheet hand over hand at a snail's pace. Terribly agitated because they were barreling down on the mark with boats at close quarters all around them, our lady skipper cried to "hurry it up" to which she received an extremely haughty, "But you said, don't make it fast!"

This is an example of the reason we are covering all the various terms which may seem confusing at first. PROPER COMMUNICATION ON A BOAT IS AN ABSOLUTE NECESSITY OR ACCIDENTS CAN RESULT.

Having jibed, as in Figure 24, we can steer any course on the starboard tack all the way up to "closehauled" just by "hardening up" and this is a good exercise in learning the feel of different points of sail.

Beating

Now, imagine we want to reach a destination that is directly upwind of us. We know by now that we can't sail closer to the wind than 45 degrees so we must zig-zag first on one tack and then on the other until we reach it. Each turn we make from port to starboard and vice-versa with the bow pointing momentarily into the wind is called a "tack", "tacking" or "coming about." A series of tacks is called a "beat" or "beating to windward."

The command of preparation for a tack is: "Stand by to come about," or, more usually, "Ready about!" Upon hearing this the crew's main job is to get the jib ready for the tack by uncleating, but not releasing it, and preparing to take in on the opposite jib sheet. The main, which is near the middle of the boat when closehauled, is of no concern because it has only a short distance to travel and the breeze carries it across automatically. The crew should say "Ready," then the skipper puts the helm (the tiller or steering wheel) over and gives the command of execution "Hard Alee!" at the same time. The latter term is an Americanization of the command "Helm's Alee!" which means the helm is put to the leeward side of the boat. The "windward" of anything is that which wind strikes first, while the "leeward" (usually pronounced "looward" is that which the wind strikes next.

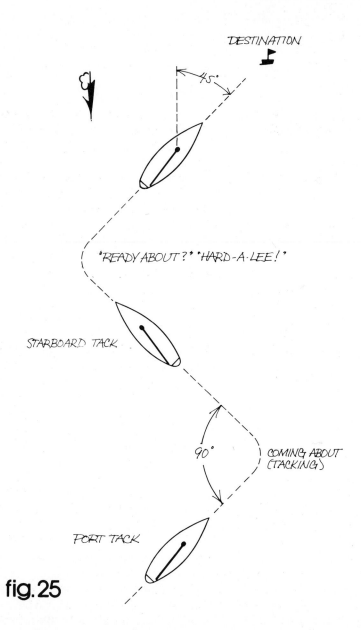

DESTINATION

45°

"READY ABOUT?" "HARD-A-LEE!"

STARBOARD TACK

90°   COMING ABOUT
                       (TACKING)

PORT TACK

fig. 25

If a beachball were being propelled by the wind across the water, the side of the boat it hits first is the windward side. Thus, the other side is the leeward side. Of two boats, the boat it hits first is the windward boat and next the leeward boat. The same holds true for windward or leeward islands, marks, or whatever object you are referring to. For instance, two boats may be approaching on a collision course, one closehauled beating to windward and the other running free. The wind is hitting the boat running downwind first so it is the "windward boat" and since it is hitting the boat beating upwind next, it is called the "leeward boat." This can seem wrong even to sailors who have a reasonable amount of experience, but is important to remember for reasons of right-of-way which will be explained later.

Returning to "tacking," whenever the tiller is put to leeward the boat turns towards the wind. When you point to the wind and turn the bow in that direction, you are tacking (when you actually change tacks). Remember the two "T's" -- *T*ack *T*owards the wind.

Sometimes the boat fails to complete a tack (or "come about") and ends up dead in the water head to wind. In other words, the bow is pointed into the wind and the boat is motionless. Without motion or "way on" there is no water flowing past the rudder. As mentioned before when discussing leaving a mooring, the rudder has to deflect water in order to turn the boat, so the "wayless" boat has no "steerageway." Turning the rudder doesn't turn the boat. A boat in this predicament is said, as explained on pages 19 and 20, to be "in irons."

Usually this happens to the inexperienced helmsman who allows the boat to slow up too much before attempting to tack. Then a wave stops the boat in the middle of the tack leaving the boat in irons. It is a temporary condition since the boat will shortly fall off to one tack or the other. The only problem is that it may not be the desired tack. If, for instance, the reason for the tack was a moored boat dead ahead, it could be very embarrassing (and costly) to get in irons and then fall back on the same tack. The boat doesn't gain steerageway until it gains speed, so by the time you speed up enough to try to tack again, you may collide with the moored boat.

The helmsman often isn't totally at fault when a boat ends up in irons. If the mainsail remains cleated during a tack and the crew doesn't get the jib trimmed in on the new tack fast enough, the main may force the boat up into the wind again. By this time the boat has lost so much forward momentum that she is in irons.

The main does not need to be uncleated when tacking, but it is a good idea for the skipper to hold the mainsheet at all times when sailing amongst moored boats. If a gust of wind hits the boat the alert skipper can release the mainsheet which spills the wind out of the main and lets the boat straighten up. In a centerboard boat this can avert a capsize.

The other way to reduce the force of the wind on the sails (which causes the boat to heel way over) is to head more into the wind and thereby luff the sails. In small doses this is called "feathering" the boat to windward, but in response to a strong gust it is simply luffing.

Circle of Courses

The foregoing has been a description of the various points of sailing. Actually whenever we turn a boat substantially we change from one point of sailing to another. If we turned the boat in a tight 360 degrees, its wake would describe a circle and we would have passed through all the points of sailing, however briefly. It is sometimes easier for the beginner to think of the boat always being on one part of the circle as in Figure 26.

As you can see in the diagrams, whenever the boat turns its sail trim will correspond to one of the positions on the "circle of courses" diagram.

You can get your boat from any course (port or starboard tack) aimed towards any specific destination by making a circle in either direction (clockwise or counterclockwise, except that you must tack your way directly upwind). Just begin by pointing the boat in the direction that is closest to the destination and make the necessary sail adjustments. When a "come about" or a "jibe" is involved there is usually a shortest way. (See Figures 28 and 29.)

Collision Avoidance

There is one matter of great importance before you go out sailing the first time: Collision avoidance. Though we will go into right-of-way rules later, it is the responsibility of the helmsman to avoid a collision. He must be constantly on the lookout for potential trouble and, though he can delegate a crew member to help keep an eye out, the ultimate responsibility is his. This means that if the boat is heeling and the sails block his view to leeward, he must occasionally peek under the boom. If another boat is heading your way there is one sure way of determining whether or not it's on a collision course. Note the bearing of the boat either by using the compass or by lining it up with some item on your boat such as a lifeline, stanchion or a shroud. If, in a short time, you take the bearing again and it hasn't changed, you are on a collision course as in Figure 30. Relative speeds of the two boats make no difference at all. You could be sailing at five knots and be on a collision course with a ship traveling at 25 knots, if the bearing doesn't change.

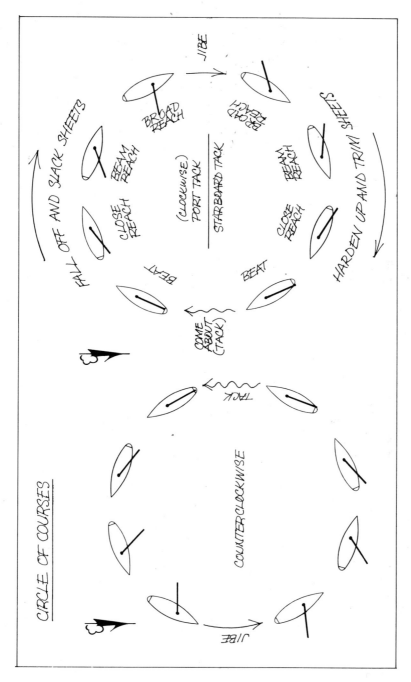

fig. 26

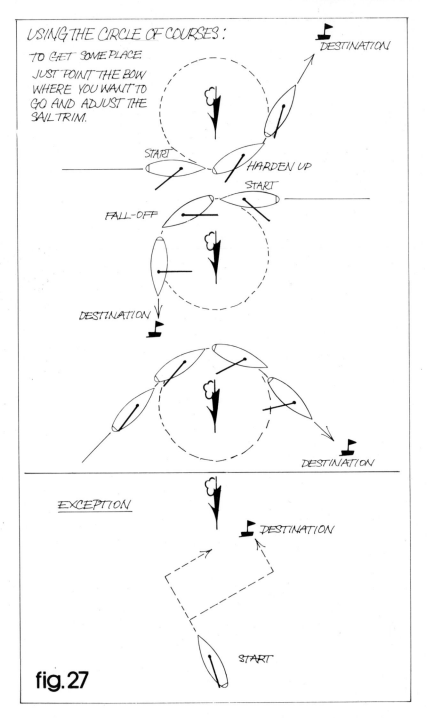

USING THE CIRCLE OF COURSES:

TO GET SOME PLACE,
JUST POINT THE BOW
WHERE YOU WANT TO
GO AND ADJUST THE
SAIL TRIM.

DESTINATION

START   HARDEN UP

START

FALL-OFF

DESTINATION

DESTINATION

EXCEPTION

DESTINATION

START

fig. 27

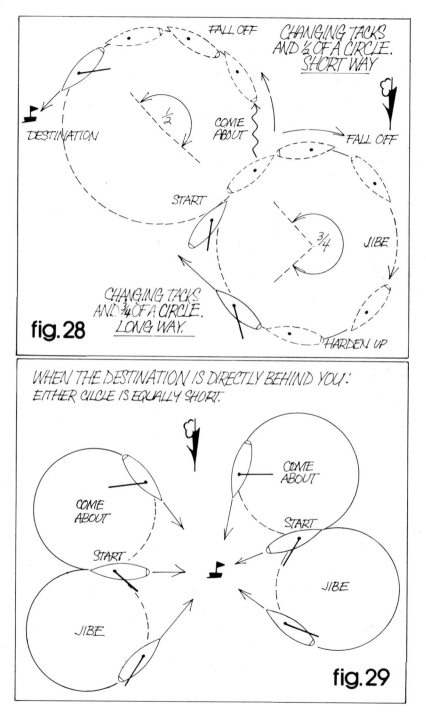

FALL OFF

CHANGING TACKS
AND ½ OF A CIRCLE.
SHORT WAY

½

COME
ABOUT

FALL OFF

DESTINATION

START

¾

JIBE

CHANGING TACKS
AND ¾ OF A CIRCLE.
LONG WAY.

fig. 28

HARDEN UP

WHEN THE DESTINATION IS DIRECTLY BEHIND YOU:
EITHER CICLE IS EQUALLY SHORT.

COME
ABOUT

COME
ABOUT

COME
ABOUT

START

START

JIBE

JIBE

fig. 29

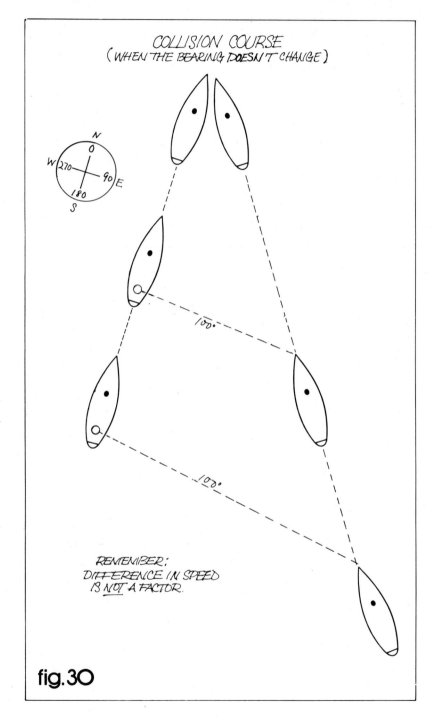

fig.30

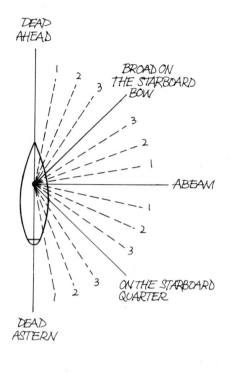

If a crew member spots a boat that may be a potential hazard, he must point it out quickly to the skipper in terms that describe its location accurately. The words in Figure 31 are those the crew member would say to indicate a hazard at the various positions.

If you want to pinpoint the location further, you describe the hazard in "points." There are 32 points in the 360 degrees of a compass (11¼ degrees for each point). The dotted lines indicate the points (eight to a quadrant). Starting from abeam, you have "1, 2 or 3 points forward of abeam" and "1, 2 or 3 points abaft abeam" (aft of abeam). There are "1, 2 or 3 points on the starboard bow" and "1, 2 or 3 points on the starboard quarter." This covers one side of the boat. The other side is exactly the same, but with "port" substituted for "starboard."

Additional Knots

The last subject covered in the first class are knots. Two have already been covered -- the "figure-eight" and the "stop" knot. One of the most useful knots you can know for sailing is the "bowline" which is pronounced "bōlin." It is used to make a non-slip loop for towing, docking, and a multitude of other purposes. Its major attribute is that no matter how

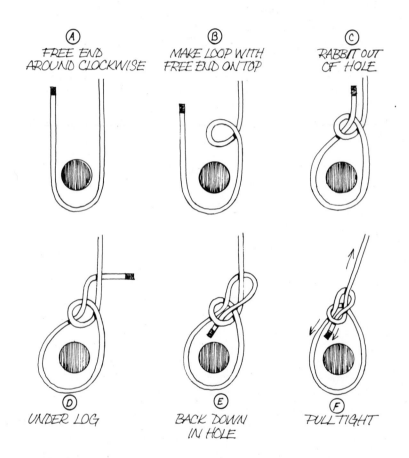

Ⓐ
FREE END
AROUND CLOCKWISE

Ⓑ
MAKE LOOP WITH
FREE END ON TOP

Ⓒ
RABBIT OUT
OF HOLE

Ⓓ
UNDER LOG

Ⓔ
BACK DOWN
IN HOLE

Ⓕ
PULL TIGHT

fig.32

much strain is put on the knot, it can be easily untied (unlike some knots that tighten up when strain is applied). Though there are many ways of teaching people how to tie it, the time-honored one has a rabbit coming out of his hole (the loop), running under a log (the standing part of the line), and going back down the hole. The object is to get the end of the line back through the loop the same way it came out. When you can tie this one in the pitch dark, on a heaving deck, with one hand, you're an old salt!

TEST QUESTIONS -- SECTION ONE

1. What is LOA?
2. What is LWL?
3. Where is beam measured?
4. What are topsides?
5. What is aspect ratio?
6. What is ballast-displacement ratio?
7. What is the difference between a ketch and a yawl?
8. Define a cutter.
9. Does a schooner have a mizzen?
10. What is the difference between standing and running rigging?
11. What is the difference between stays and shrouds?
12. What is the difference between halyards and sheets?
13. What are the names of the three corners of a sail?
14. What are the edge areas between the corners called?
15. What is the extra material in a convex sail called?
16. What is freeboard?
17. What corner of the jib is attached first?
18. Name three ways of recognizing the above corner?
19. Which sail do you raise first?
20. Describe a boat that is in irons.
21. What are telltales?
22. What are the commands when tacking? Jibing?
23. What is the location of the main boom on a starboard tack run?
24. What is a beat?
25. What is luffing?
26. What is hardening up?
27. What is by-the-lee?
28. What is leeward?
29. Why should you be ready to release the mainsheet in a hurry on a centerboard boat?
30. How do you know if you're on a collision course?
31. If a crew told you there was a boat on your starboard quarter, where would you look?

SAILS AND WIND

In recent years a great deal has been learned about the relationship between wind and sails. For a long time people thought the wind just pushed the sails. Even though this force was sideways when closehauled, the wedge shape of the keel was supposed to squirt the boat forward. Though not entirely accurate, the theory isn't too far off. The wind exerts both a sideways force and a forward pull on the sail. In simplest terms, the keel keeps the boat from slipping sideways, so all that is left is the forward pull.

The forward pull is caused by air flowing over the surface of the sail as it does over an airplane wing. Air splits as it passes on either side of an

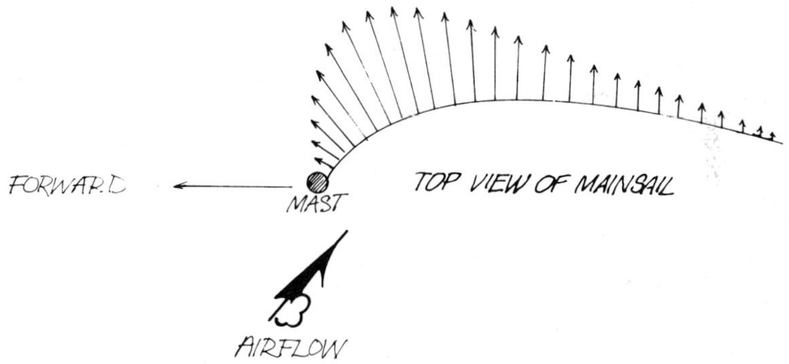

FORWARD ⟵—— ● MAST   TOP VIEW OF MAINSAIL

AIRFLOW

fig. 33

airplane wing. Because of the curvature of the upper surface of the wing, the air passing over that side has to travel a greater distance than that passing under the wing. Since it has to go farther, it has to go faster in order to reach the trailing edge at the same time as the air flowing past the underside of the wing. Daniel Bernoulli discovered in 1738 that this increased velocity meant a corresponding decrease in atmospheric pressure, i.e., suction. This suction acts at right angles to the surface and the amount of suction can be diagrammed as in Figure 33. The longest arrows represent the greatest suction. The higher the velocity on both sides, the greater the suction; and the greater the difference in velocity between the sides, the greater the suction.

The air has to flow over the surface smoothly and evenly, though. Once the air starts to "separate" from the surface it becomes turbulent. Instead of an even flow, burbles develop that reduce suction. Much of the turbulence is caused by the angle that the airfoil makes with the airflow. This is called the "angle of attack" or "angle of incidence." If the angle is small as pictured in Figure 34A the airflow remains "attached" to the surface for quite a distance back towards the leech of the sail or the trailing edge of a wing. When the angle is increased as in Figure 34B, the

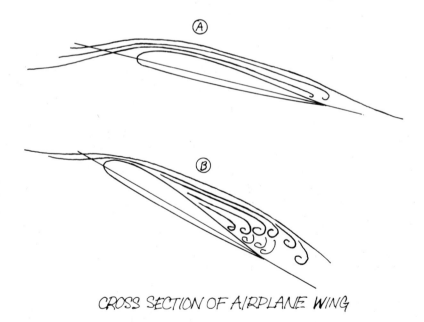

CROSS SECTION OF AIRPLANE WING

fig.34

airflow detaches earlier and turbulence works its way forward. At a certain angle and speed there is so much separation of flow that the wing no longer develops enough suction or "lift" and a stall occurs. In an airplane the result is dramatic since the aircraft will drop suddenly. A sailboat, however, will just heel over more and slow down.

Up to the stall point, however, the greater the angle of attack the greater the lift derived. Imagine the wing in Figure 34A as symmetrical, instead of asymmetrical. All other lifting surfaces of a yacht are symmetrical -- the keel, hull, centerboard and rudder. Yet they can still develop lift because of the angle the water hits them, the angle of attack, as we will see later in the chapter on Hull and Sails. In the diagram, the air hitting the underside of the wing travels a lesser distance than that which has to travel around the leading edge and over the top, so suction develops. In addition, the deflection of the air or water is like the lift a child's hand gets when he sticks it out of a car window and tilts it upward.

A man told me one time that he and his friends, newly introduced to the sport of sailing, decided to forego all nautical lingo in favor of flying terms. He claimed they were much more descriptive. For instance, he said when the sail luffed they would say, "Pull it in, it's stalling."

As we can see from the foregoing, they had their terms backwards. The sail stalls if it is trimmed in too tight. If a sail is eased to the point just before it luffs, we can be certain it isn't stalled and is properly trimmed. A luff is easy to see because the leading edge of the sail is flapping. *A stalled sail, however, looks the same as one operating at maximum efficiency.*

So that's the reason for the basic rule of sail trimming: EASE THE SAIL UNTIL IT LUFFS AND THEN TRIM IT IN JUST ENOUGH TO STOP THE LUFF. This is a good rule for beginners, but after you have sailed for a while you may find, especially on reaches, the need to trim in a little past this point to get maximum drive from the sail. The judgement depends a great deal on wind strength. In lighter winds you can trim in tighter before separation and turbulence occurs. Of course, the tighter you trim in, the more sideways is the driving force. So although greater than before, it may be transmitted more into detrimental heeling than into beneficial forward driving force.

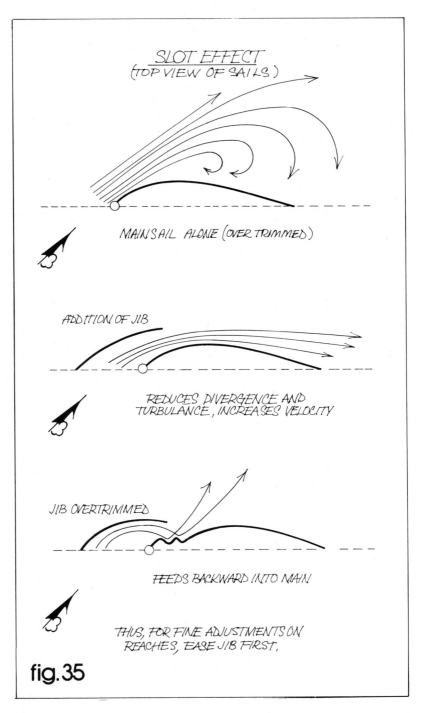

SLOT EFFECT
(TOP VIEW OF SAILS)

MAINSAIL ALONE (OVER TRIMMED)

ADDITION OF JIB

REDUCES DIVERGENCE AND
TURBULANCE, INCREASES VELOCITY

JIB OVERTRIMMED

FEEDS BACKWARD INTO MAIN

THUS, FOR FINE ADJUSTMENTS ON
REACHES, EASE JIB FIRST,

fig. 35

Slot Effect

Boats with jibs have added advantages over those without. First, the jib is a very efficient sail since there is no mast in front of it to disrupt the airflow. Second, it bends and funnels the air behind the main. The funneling action tends to increase the speed of the air flowing past the leeward side of the main. This, because of Bernoulli's Principle, increases the suction and efficiency of the main. As we have mentioned before, the faster the air travels, the less it can bend around the sail curvature. Luckily, the jib not only speeds up the air, but bends it aft so it can follow the main curvature more easily. This velocity increase and bending is called "slot effect," the "slot" being the opening between the main and the jib. The result is that though a boat can sail under just mainsail or just the jib, the combination of main *and* jib add up to greater effectiveness than the sum of each alone.

Heeling

For many reasons, some of which will be covered later, "heeling" is an enemy to the sailor. If a boat is closehauled, the sail trimmed in tight, many of the force arrows point sideways, as in Figure 36A. In other words, there is a large sideways push resulting in the boat heeling (leaning over). As the sail is eased out for a reach (Figure 36B) the arrows start to line up more with the course of the boat. The result is less heeling and more forward pull. A reach, therefore, is usually the fastest point of sailing.

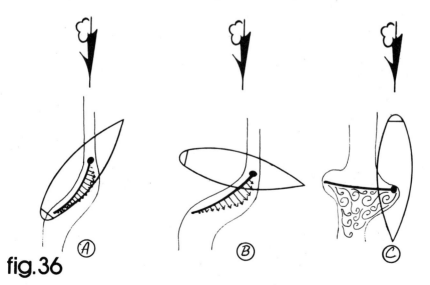

fig.36 Ⓐ   Ⓑ   Ⓒ

It may appear that you're sailing faster when closehauled, because there's a great deal of commotion. The boat is heeling over, plowing through the seas, and the wind seems stronger because you're moving towards it. When you fall off to a reach, the commotion quiets down. You're sailing across the wind and the sea and neither seems as powerful. The boat is more upright because the pull of the sails is more forward. Carrying this one step further, you might think that a run would be even faster because the wind and the boat are both going in the same direction. On a run, though, the wind can't flow over both sides of the sail which is necessary for any suction to develop on the leeward side of the sail. So the wind is just pushing the boat. As you can see in Figure 36C there is pure turbulence behind the sail downwind. Were a jib present it would be "blanketed" by the main; i.e., no wind would be reaching it because of the main being in between it and the wind.

When the wind velocity increases to the point where a given boat on a reach is "overpowered," heeling excessively in comparison to forward drive, a faster point of sailing would then be a run.

Wind Shifts

For the highest efficiency, sails must be adjusted so they make just the proper angle to the wind. Since the wind is constantly changing direction, this means the sails must be constantly adjusted to the various shifts.

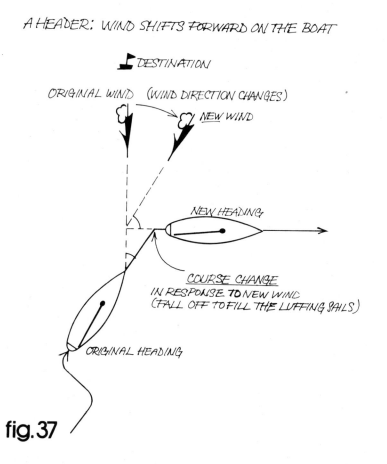

A HEADER: WIND SHIFTS FORWARD ON THE BOAT

DESTINATION

ORIGINAL WIND (WIND DIRECTION CHANGES)

NEW WIND

NEW HEADING

COURSE CHANGE
IN RESPONSE TO NEW WIND
(FALL OFF TO FILL THE LUFFING SAILS)

ORIGINAL HEADING

fig.37

A shift of the "true" wind direction, the actual wind, is called either a "header" or a "lift" depending on the relationship of the shift to the heading of the boat. Figure 37 shows a boat closehauled on the port tack. If the wind shifts more towards the bow of the boat, causing the sails to luff, necessitating a change of course away from the wind to keep them filled, the boat has been "headed" or has "sailed into a header."

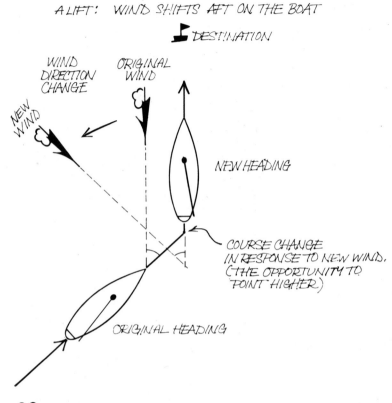

A LIFT: WIND SHIFTS AFT ON THE BOAT

DESTINATION

WIND DIRECTION CHANGE

ORIGINAL WIND

NEW WIND

NEW HEADING

COURSE CHANGE IN RESPONSE TO NEW WIND. (THE OPPORTUNITY TO POINT HIGHER.)

ORIGINAL HEADING

fig. 38

If the wind shifts more towards the stern of the boat, allowing the skipper to steer higher than before, he has been "lifted" or is sailing "in a lift."

A header or a lift occurring on a reach means a corresponding sail adjustment -- trimming for a header and easing for a lift -- while maintaining a constant heading.

A wind shift that is a header for a boat on a port tack is a lift for a boat on the starboard tack. The boat sailing on a lift will reach his desired

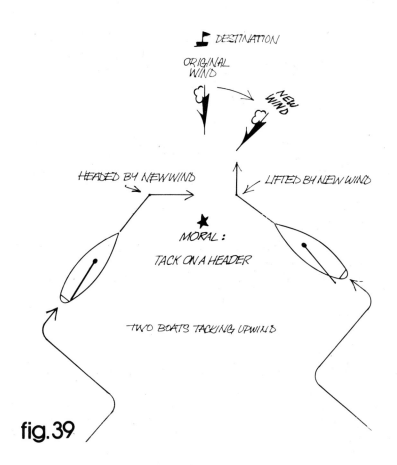

DESTINATION

ORIGINAL
WIND

NEW WIND

HEADED BY NEW WIND

LIFTED BY NEW WIND

MORAL:

TACK ON A HEADER

TWO BOATS TACKING UPWIND

fig.39

upwind destination faster than one sailing in a header. A standard sailboat racing axiom, therefore, is "if you're headed, tack."

When a wind shift is described in relation to a compass direction, it is said to be "veering" or "backing." A veering wind is one that is shifting clockwise.

For instance, a wind that shifts from north to northeast is "veering." A shift from east to northeast is "backing" in that the shift is counterclockwise. A north wind is one that blows from the north. Don't confuse this with *current* which is named for the direction *to* which it flows. A northerly current is one that flows from the south.

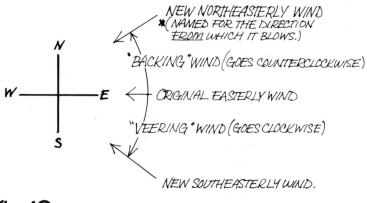

fig.40

The foregoing shifts are changes in the direction of the actual wind blowing over the water. Another type of shift, which also causes the need for sail adjustment is a change in the "apparent wind" direction.

Apparent Wind

"Apparent wind" is a very simple concept that continues to mystify many people who have been sailing for years.

It is the resultant wind derived from the wind produced by the boat moving through the air and the wind produced by nature -- the "true wind." Thus, it is the wind you feel on the boat. Cigarette smoke, telltales, electronic wind direction indicators of cruising boats all show the apparent wind direction. We often get the comment from people the first time out, "You said we sail within 45 degrees of the wind when closehauled, but the wool on the shrouds indicates we're sailing almost into the wind." This is their first experience with apparent wind on a sailboat.

Imagine yourself standing up in a convertible. It is a calm day, so there's no true wind. As the convertible starts forward, you will begin to feel a breeze on your face that increases as the speed of the car increases. At 10 mph you will feel a 10 mph breeze on your face. This is apparent wind.

Now imagine yourself in the same car heading north and there's an easterly wind of 10 mph blowing. It is hitting the right side of your face. As the car starts forward you will not feel two different winds, one on the side and one on the front of your face, but a resultant wind coming from an angle forward of the true wind.

By drawing, to a consistent scale, a parallelogram from the boat speed and the true wind, you can determine the force and direction of the apparent wind. Let's say your boat tacks in 80 degrees. That means the true wind is 40 degrees off your bow. If, for example, the boat speed is six knots and the true wind is twelve knots, measure off the units. Then draw a parallelogram, the diagonal of which is the apparent wind. By measuring the length of the diagonal, you can determine the speed in knots of the apparent wind.

In this example (see Figure 41) it is 17 knots, and bears 27 degrees from your heading versus 40 degrees for the true wind. Notice how the direction of the apparent wind changes with the true wind in the following diagrams. (For the purposes of these diagrams we'll keep true wind speed and boat speed constant, which would only be the case at different points of sailing if the boats were different sizes.)

There are four points that are obvious from these diagrams. First, the apparent wind is always forward of the true wind (unless the true wind is dead ahead or astern). Second, as the true wind comes aft, the apparent wind lessens in velocity. Third, when the true wind is well aft, a small change in true wind direction makes a large change in apparent wind direction. And fourth, when the boat is on a beam reach or closehauled, the apparent wind is of greater velocity than the true wind.

The first point is important when considering when to jibe. Since it is desirable to sail at the slight angle to the wind rather than dead downwind, you may not be heading to your desired destination and will have to jibe to reach it. It's important, therefore, to determine the direction of the true wind and the angle your heading is making with it. If you know you are steering 20 degrees from dead downwind on one tack, then you will be on the same point of sailing when you are 20 degrees from dead downwind on the other tack. The point of jibing should come when your destination bears 40 degrees off your bow from your present heading. The key, of course, is determining the direction of the true wind. By glancing at your telltales and at the wind signs on the water -- like streaks and ripples -- you can judge about how far aft of the apparent wind the true wind is.

A more positive way of determining true wind direction is by heading off momentarily until the apparent wind and the true wind line up, i.e., dead downwind. The difference between the new heading and your former heading, 20 degrees in the example above, when doubled (40°), is the number of degrees in which you'll jibe.

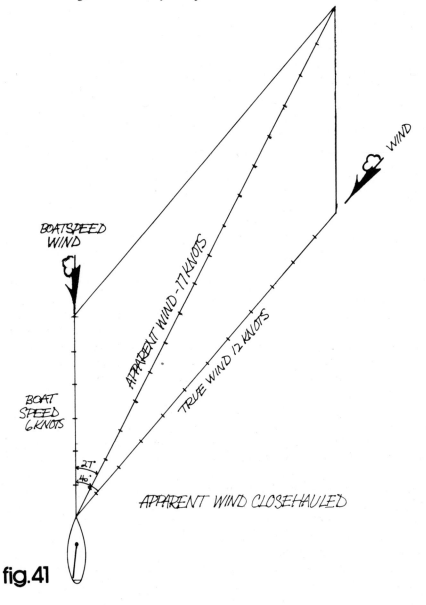

fig.41

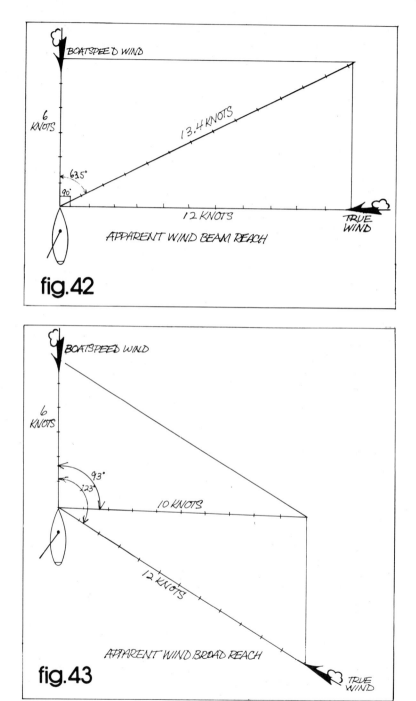

BOATSPEED WIND

6 KNOTS

13.4 KNOTS

63.5°

90°

12 KNOTS

TRUE WIND

APPARENT WIND BEAM REACH

fig.42

BOATSPEED WIND

6 KNOTS

93°

123°

10 KNOTS

12 KNOTS

APPARENT WIND BROAD REACH

TRUE WIND

fig.43

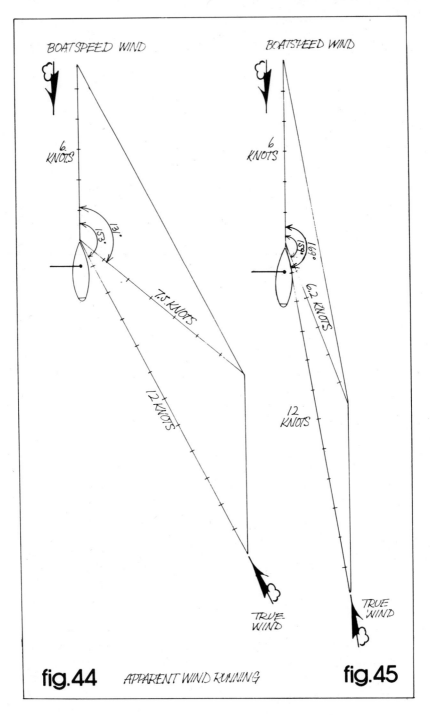

BOATSPEED WIND

6 KNOTS

131°

153°

7.5 KNOTS

12 KNOTS

TRUE WIND

fig.44   *APPARENT WIND RUNNING*

BOATSPEED WIND

6 KNOTS

169°

153°

6.2 KNOTS

12 KNOTS

TRUE WIND

fig.45

The second point, that as that true wind comes aft, the apparent wind speed lessens, is obvious if you have ever seen powerboats head downwind. Sometimes they cruise along at the same speed and direction as the true wind. Their exhaust hangs around the boat, an enveloping cloud (one reason we sail!), and the apparent wind is just about zero.

This lessening of the wind speed you feel on the boat and thereby the force of the wind on the sails can lull you into forgetting the difference when you round a mark and start on a beat. You may have started your sailing outing on a run, so you had no idea of the apparent wind strength on a beat. Or the wind may have increased during the run. Either way you must consider the possibility that you many have to shorten sail on a cruising boat when you come up on a beat, and it is easiest to change jibs while still on the run. Let's say a boat is going nine knots in a 16 knot breeze. If dead downwind the apparent wind is the true wind minus the boat speed, or just seven knots. This doesn't feel like much wind and the force on the sails is relatively light. When the boat starts beating she may slow down to six knots, but the apparent wind increases to almost 21 knots. You would assume that since the apparent wind is now three times greater than the downwind velocity, it exerts three times the force against the sails. Wrong. The force of the wind *quadruples* as the velocity doubles, so the wind force is *nine times greater* on the closehauled course than on the run in this case. Couple this with the increased heeling moment of the closehauled course, and the boat many very well be overpowered. You should have had the forethought during the run to shorten sail.

The third point we made about the apparent wind diagrams was that, when the true wind was well aft, a small change in true wind direction makes a large change in apparent wind direction. Compare Figure 43 with Figure 44. A 30 degree change in true wind direction made a 38 degree change in apparent wind. In comparing Figure 44 with Figure 45, we find a 16 degree change in true wind makes a 28 degree change in apparent wind. This, among other things, is what makes steering dead downwind so difficult. A small swing by the lee actually results in an exaggerated swing of the apparent wind by the lee. This can cause oscillation as the apparent wind swings madly back and forth from one side of the boat to the other on relatively minor changes in heading. At worst, it can force a flying jibe on the inexperienced helmsman.

The fourth point was that when a boat is reaching or beating, the apparent wind is of greater velocity than the true wind. You are, in effect, "making your own wind." In iceboating it is an important part of the resulting high speeds. The speed record for iceboats is over 140 mph. The wind was probably around 50 mph. So obviously it was "created" wind. The faster the boat went, the higher the wind velocity it created. Only because of the lack of friction can these high speeds be attained. A normal sailboat is limited in speed by hull resistance, skin friction and wave making drag, so it cannot take full advantage of the increased apparent wind velocity. A planing sailboat is more apt to get up on a high-speed plane on a reach than a run just because of this apparent wind increase. Even so, the faster a boat is to windward, the more closewinded (able to head close to the wind) it must be.

In the first set of wind diagrams, everything remained constant except the direction of the true wind which was moved further aft in each subsequent diagram. Now let us change the boat speed and the wind velocity keeping the true wind direction at 45 degrees off the bow.

Notice in Figure 46 that initially the wind speed was 10 knots and the boat speed four knots. The dotted extension of the true wind line indicates a four knot increase or puff. So we see a basic axiom: "In a puff the apparent wind comes aft." To be correct this necessitates a constant speed on the boat's part. Generally, however, by the time the boat picks up speed the puff has passed, so the axiom holds true.

We already know that we point higher in order to reduce heeling when hit by an overpowering gust. This axiom shows another reason to do the same thing. As the gust hits the apparent wind goes aft causing more heeling and less drive and changing the angle of incidence, the angle the apparent wind makes with the sails, so that the sails now are improperly trimmed unless you head up or ease sheets or traveler. This change in apparent wind direction is important to remember even on light days. On days when you have a three mph breeze, the wind velocity in a puff is apt to be more than double the regular breeze. When it is blowing 15 mph, gusts may get to only 20-22 mph or about a third higher. Thus, the change in apparent wind direction aft is often greater on light days than on heavy ones.

The dot-dash lines in the diagram show the resulting change in apparent wind when the wind dies suddenly. With the boat speed remaining constant and the wind velocity lowering to six knots, the apparent wind goes forward. This is one of the reasons that small catamarans rarely carry spinnakers. The hulls have very little resistance to the water, and downwind the cats sail almost as fast as the wind making it very difficult to keep a spinnaker drawing. If the wind dies for a moment, the spinnaker collapses and it is very difficult to get it filled until the boat slows down. Therefore, small cats, much like iceboats, tack downwind by jibing. By sailing from reach to reach they pick up greater speed and make up the extra distance sailed.

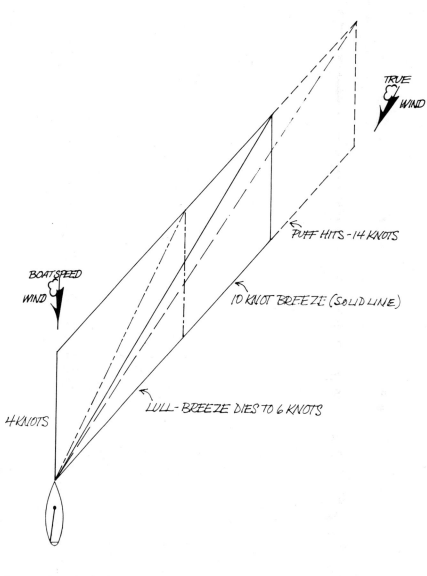

TRUE WIND

PUFF HITS – 14 KNOTS

BOAT SPEED

WIND

10 KNOT BREEZE (SOLID LINE)

LULL – BREEZE DIES TO 6 KNOTS

4 KNOTS

fig.46

458

458

SAIL TRIM

To sail well, we must allow for the shifts in the true and apparent wind and still maintain the optimum drive angle of the wind to the sails by both judicious helmsmanship and proper sail trim. By imagining the air flowing past the sails as smoke, one can get a much better idea of proper sail trim. Many wind tunnel tests (called "smoke visualization tests") have been done with smoke blowing past sails. The difference between smooth flow and turbulent flow is very easy to see. Obviously we can't create a smoke-screen in front of our sailboat, but we can do the next best thing: attach telltales to the sails so they indicate whether the flow past the sail is turbulent or smooth.

This has been done very successfully with jibs and has been tried on mainsails with much less success. The most practical method is to thread a needle with some light wool of a high visibility color and pass it through the sail. Cut it off leaving about five inches to hang out on either side of the sail and tie two small overhand knots right next to the sailcloth so the wool won't pull through. By using a long piece of wool, pulling it right through to five inches from the end, and cutting it off five inches from the cloth, you can repeat the process at other points on the sail without having to rethread the needle. Another good practice is to place the wool higher on one side of the sail than on the other. In certain sunlight conditions it's hard to tell which piece of wool is which unless they are at different levels. Some people place tape on either side of the sail in fear that the needle hole will weaken the material, but the edges of the tape tend to loosen and the wool hangs up on them and on its adhesive. Eventually the tape comes off anyway, so it's best not to use it in the first place.

The telltales should be placed in three positions along the luff of the jib about six to twelve inches from the leading edge depending on the size of the boat. Make sure that the wool cannot touch a seam or any sail stitching, because the hairs of the wool will catch on anything rough. A type of wool should be used that has as few tiny hairs as possible. Though Angora wool makes the best shroud telltales because of its mass to weight

63

ratio (being very light and fuzzy), it is definitely not the type to use next to a sailcloth which the fuzz hangs up on.

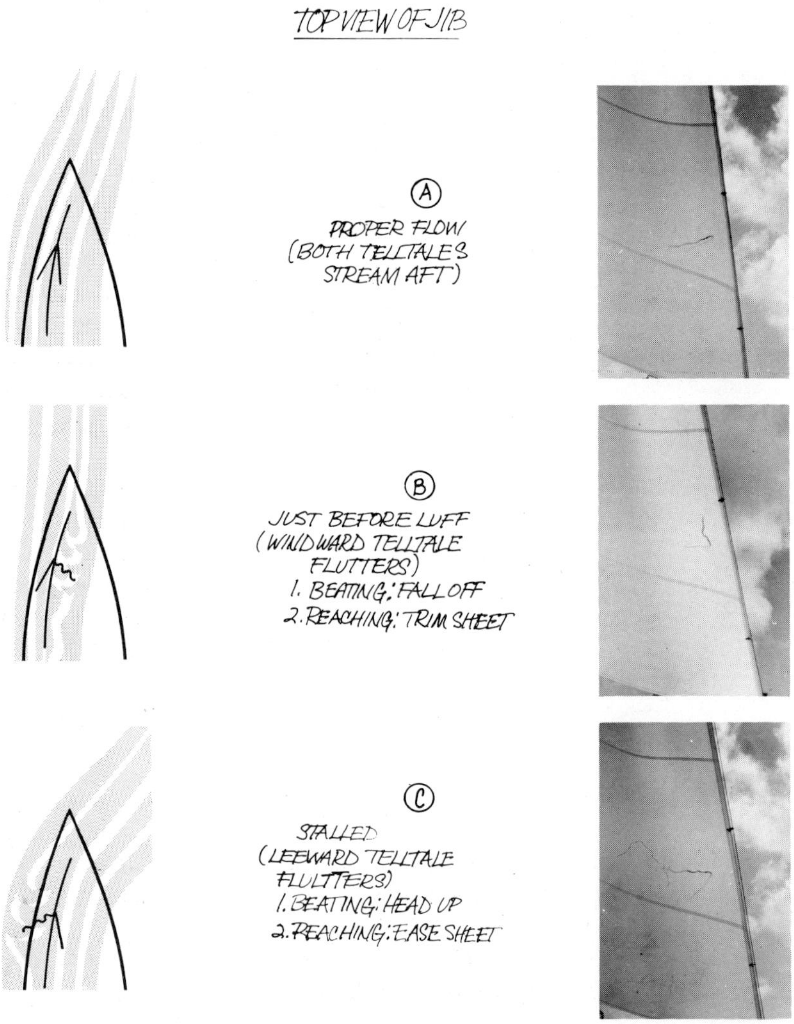

TOP VIEW OF JIB

(A)
PROPER FLOW
(BOTH TELLTALES
STREAM AFT)

(B)
JUST BEFORE LUFF
(WINDWARD TELLTALE
FLUTTERS)
1. BEATING: FALL OFF
2. REACHING: TRIM SHEET

(C)
STALLED
(LEEWARD TELLTALE
FLUTTERS)
1. BEATING: HEAD UP
2. REACHING: EASE SHEET

fig.47

Now watch the middle set of telltales on the jib as you change your heading without varying your jib trim. In Figures 47A and B, you will notice that as the boat heads up towards the wind, the windward telltales will start to flutter. Conversely, when the boat heads too far off the wind, as in Figure 47C, the leeward telltale flutters because the angle of incidence (angle of attack) becomes so great that the wind is hitting mostly on the windward side of the sail. This disrupts the flow over the lee side and turbulence results. To the sailor this is most important. If there is turbulence on the lee side, the sail, as an airfoil, is stalled and thereby does not produce the desired drive. Again, a luff is easy to see because the sail starts to flutter, but a stall isn't. We've said before that the greater the angle of attack, the greater the drive until separation begins. With the jib telltales described (plus a few others further back on the sail) we can trim the jib until the leeward telltales start to flutter. You'll find it's a very fine line between a luff and a stall, probably between a 5 to 10 degree change in heading or angle of attack.

Telltales are very helpful for the beginner and yet can be used to advantage by the expert. The sailor who is beginning to learn to sail to windward, by using these telltales, may use a very simple rule (dubbed "Reinhorn's Law" in honor of Dr. Reinhorn -- an Offshore Sailing School student of 1967). The rule reads, "Point the tiller at the fluttering piece of wool." If the leeward wool is fluttering, it's because the boat is being sailed too "hard," too far away from the wind for the desired closehauled course, and should be pointed more towards the wind. Putting the tiller to leeward cures this. If the windward piece of wool is fluttering the boat is being sailed too close to the wind, on the verge of a luff. Putting the tiller to windward causes the boat to fall off and solves the problem.

There are some top skippers who consider these telltales a crutch for incompetence, because they have learned to sail properly without them. They have a point when you are sailing closehauled and the skipper is steering entirely by wool on the jib. One of the mistakes that many skippers make is trying to keep the jib completely full without allowing the windward (or leeward) piece of wool to flutter. There are many conditions, however, when this shouldn't be done. For instance, in a strong wind and smooth sea you may be able to "pinch" (carry a very slight luff in the jib) and still maintain your speed or even go faster. If you fall off until the sail is full, excessive heeling reduces the speed of the boat. So the experienced helmsman takes the wool on the jib with a grain of salt and steers what he feels to be the fastest course for the existing conditions.

There are two conditions when the jib telltales really come into their own. The first is reaching. While racing the jib should be "played" constantly on a reach. This means a crew member must ease it when it stalls and trim it when it luffs. He should have his eyes glued to the telltales near the luff of the sail and the jib sheet in his hand whether a small boat or a Twelve Meter. Without the wool on the jib it is *very, very* difficult to determine if the sail is stalled.

As with everything else about sailing, there are exceptions. When the reach becomes very broad and approaches a run, there is a transition, in simplest terms, from "pull" to "push." Instead of flow over the lee side of the sail we have strictly "drag." The sail form that creates the most drag will push the boat fastest. Though we want to retain aerodynamic flow over the lee side as long as possible, at some point near a run it is no longer possible. After that point sail curvature is no longer helpful and "projected area" is the most important factor. Projected area is just the amount of sail area exposed to the wind. Just as a large parachute will lower a man more gently than a small one, a large sail will push the boat faster than a small one downwind. The lee telltales which have been flowing aft start to flutter as you reach this point. Easing the sail more doesn't seem to help much, and in fact will hurt your speed because you lose sail area (Figure 48B). In practicality, a spinnaker would probably be set before this point or the jib "winged" out to the other side of the boat on a pole as in Figure 48C.

The second, and even more important use, is to determine the fore and aft placement of the jib "fair lead" or "lead." On almost all sailboats, the block on either side of the boat through which the jib sheets lead is adjustable so that it can travel six inches to a foot towards the bow or stern and be locked in any spot along the track. It is this lead that determines the shape of the jib. If it is too far forward the foot of the jib is too loose and the leech too tight, because most of the pull on the jib sheet is downward. If it is too far aft, the foot is too tight and the leech too loose because of the backward pull. What we want is a compromise between the two extremes, so that the sail is not distorted. There should be an even flow of air on both sides of the sail at all levels along the luff. In other word, the sail should have a constant angle of attack to the apparent wind. If the lead is too far forward, the bottom of the sail will have a big curve in it and the lower luff will line up with the wind before the upper part does and will luff first. Conversely, if the lead is too far aft, the leech will be loose and tend to fall off up high, causing the sail to luff first at the top. So the test to determine proper jib lead placement is to head the boat up slowly until the jib begins to luff. If it luffs at the top first the lead is too far aft. If it luffs at the bottom first, it's too far forward. But if it luffs the full length of the sail all at the same time, it's set in the right spot.

The wool telltales on the jib are more sensitive to angle change than the jib itself. In other words, you can see the windward one flutter before you can see the sail start to shake along the luff. If you have three sets of these telltales, as recommended before, you can see which one flutters first and whether your jib leads are in the right place. The telltales also allow you to make the same lead judgement by watching for a stall. If the

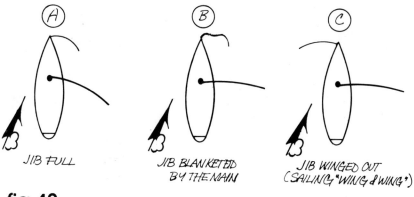

JIB FULL

JIB BLANKETED BY THE MAIN

JIB WINGED OUT (SAILING "WING & WING")

fig.48

bottom leeward one flutters first, the bottom of the sail is stalled, meaning that the sail is too flat at the bottom because the jib lead is too far aft. Thus, while racing, your crew can more readily catch a change in the situation due to an increase or decrease in wind velocity and change the jib leads fore or aft accordingly.

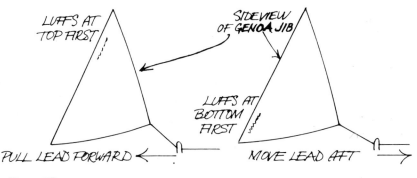

LUFFS AT TOP FIRST

SIDE VIEW OF GENOA JIB

LUFFS AT BOTTOM FIRST

PULL LEAD FORWARD ←

MOVE LEAD AFT →

fig.49

Experiment to reduce "twists" and curling of the leech to windward, so that, when pinched, jib luffs all up and down the forestay at the same time.

A Synopsis of Adjustments that can be Made to the Trim of Your Boat While Underway to Make it go Faster

Outhaul: adjusts the tension along the foot of the mainsail
    Upwind: medium -- calm day
    Downwind: loose -- any day
    Too tight: hard fold in the sail along the foot, "crow's foot" (radial folds stemming from the clew), wrinkles
    Too loose: puckers (small vertical fingers above the boom)

Downhaul: adjusts the tension along the luff of the mainsail
    Upwind: medium -- calm day
        taut -- breezy day
    Downwind: loose -- any day
    Too tight: hard fold in the sail along the luff
    Too loose: puckers (small horizontal wrinkles behind the mast)

Jib Cloth Downhaul (or jib halyard): adjusts tension along the jib luff
    Upwind: tight -- any day
    Downwind: loose -- any day
    Too tight: hard fold along the luff
    Too loose: "crow's feet" coming aft from the hanks

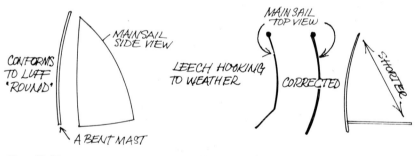

fig.50

Adjustable Backstay: under tension -- Bends mast, flattens sail and frees leech
    Upwind: medium -- calm day
        tight -- breezy day
    Downwind: loose -- any day

Boom Vang: reduces "twist" by pulling down on outboard end of boom
  Breezy day: tight -- especially reaches
  Calm day: medium -- only on reaches
  Flat day with chop: tight -- only on runs

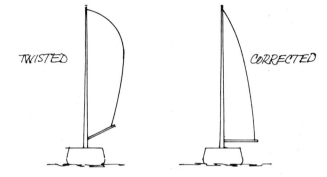

fig.51

Main Traveler: controls angle of attack of mainsail
  Upwind: in -- calm day
    out -- breezy day
  Downwind: not applicable

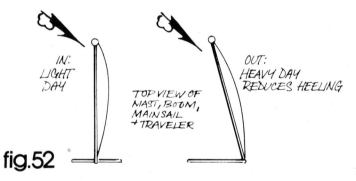

fig.52

Jib Fairleads: control angle of attack of jib and opening of "slot"
  Strong breeze: out -- reduces heeling, aft to open slot
  Light breeze: in -- point higher, forward as sheet is eased (to attain
    fullness in the sail) causing the clew to lift.

Cunningham Lines: serve as an additional downhaul when the boom is down
to the "black band," a line painted near the base of class racing boats to
limit the sail area carried. This keeps the draft moving aft in the sail on
a breezy day (see Figure 53).

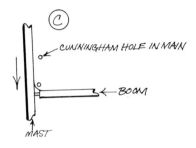

fig.53

Stopping a Sailboat

Unfortunately, a sailboat doesn't have the brakes of a car or the reverse of
a powerboat to aid it in stopping. The only way a sailboat can stop is by
heading into the wind. Sure, you can luff your sails and this will slow you
down, but you won't come to a complete stop unless you head directly
into the wind. And even when you point the boat (called "shooting" the
boat) directly into the wind, you won't come to an immediate stop but
will gradually slow down.

In order to stop alongside a man who has fallen overboard or come to a
stop with your bow at a mooring buoy, you must judge how far the boat
will shoot. Pick an imaginary spot dead downwind of your objective to be
your "turning point." The distance between this point and your objective
will vary greatly with different wind and wave conditions and with
different hull types. The stronger the wind, the shorter the distance you
can shoot. The boat stops faster because of the great resistance of the
flapping sails and the rigging to the wind and because waves are usually
higher in heavy winds and tend to stop the boat faster. In lighter airs it
will take longer for the boat to stop even though it's going slower, so allow
more room.
The approach to the turning point that allows the most flexibility is a
reach. If you approach closehauled and there's a windshift, you may have
to tack to get there. If you approach on a run, first it's difficult to judge
the turning point accurately and spin up into the wind and second, you
cannot ease the mainsail to reduce speed. On a reach, however, you have
both speed control and directional control. You can luff or trim the sails for

more or less speed and you can head up or fall off to adjust your approach to the turning point. As you round up into the wind, free the sheets and let the sails luff completely lest you back the jib accidently which forces the bow away from the wind. From the turning point to the buoy it is best not to be headed directly into the wind. Stay pointing 10°-20° towards the desired tack with sails luffing. If you miss the mooring all you need to do is trim in the sails and fall off slightly to get moving again. There is no chance of falling off accidently onto the wrong tack towards other moored boats with this method.

If you find that you have misjudged the turning point and are approaching the mooring or pier too fast, push the mainsail out against the wind. In other words, with the bow still headed into the wind, push the boom out at right angles to the boat. This is called "backing the main" and will slow the boat very quickly. As a matter of fact, if you continue to hold the boom out after the boat has stopped, the boat will start sailing backwards. Practice this. To sail well is to have complete control over the sailboat at all times. Learn how to sail the boat backwards by backing the main and jib and reverse use of the rudder. It is very satisfying to be able to make a fancy landing like rounding up into the wind to windward of a pier and backing in alongside. I wouldn't advise it without a great deal of practice, though.

Man Overboard

Should a crew member fall overboard, the first thing to do is toss him a piece of life saving equipment -- a life ring or anything that floats (and is soft in case your aim is so good you hit him). Make sure the item is not tied to the boat because you will quickly drag it out of reach of the poor person you are attempting to rescue. Next, get any sail down, such as a spinnaker, that would prevent turning the boat back. Then, if you are on a closehauled course, jibe around, aim at your turning point and shoot into the wind to come alongside (Figure 54A). The jibe is faster than a tack and takes you downwind. If you are reaching, the jibe is still faster, but you may want to play it safe and tack if it's blowing hard. If you're on a run, however, the only reasonable course is to harden up to closehauled and then tack for the turning point, as in Figure 54B. A jibe would be a useless maneuver, since you'd have to harden up anyway on the other tack. So don't believe the man that tells you one should *always* jibe to pick up a man overboard!

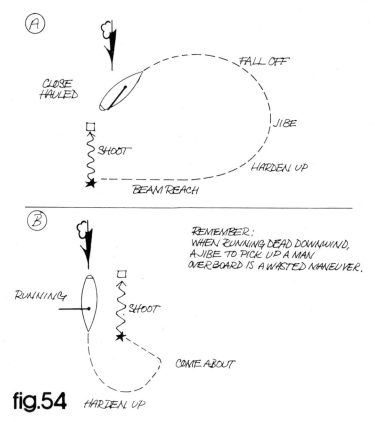

fig.54   *HARDEN UP*

TEST QUESTIONS -- SECTION TWO

1. What is slot effect?
2. What is the fastest point of sailing in light air?
3. What is a header?
4. What is a lift?
5. What is the difference between a veering and a backing wind?
6. What is apparent wind?
7. Is apparent wind always stronger than the true wind?
8. What happens to the apparent wind in a puff?
9. If you head slowly into the wind and the top telltale on the jib starts to flutter on the windward side before the lower two, what does this mean to you and how do you correct it?
10. On what point of sail should you approach a mooring?
11. What should you do first if a man falls overboard?
12. Do you always jibe around to pick up a man overboard?

STABILITY

Stability is one of the most important aspects of sailing. The force of the wind in the sails of a boat tends to heel it over and without some way of counteracting this force, the boat would tip over. The greater the ability of the boat to stay upright, the more wind force she can absorb and, all else being equal, the faster she can go. However, things are never equal. If you put a heavier keel on the boat to keep it more upright, the gain you get in being able to stand up to more wind force might be offset by the increased weight of the boat which sinks the hull deeper in the water and makes it push more volume of water aside -- increased resistance from increased displacement (weight of the boat).

Weight in the keel is not the only thing that keeps the boat upright. Hull form is also a factor. A wide flat hull will have more stability than a narrow one. Imagine a raft that is six feet wide and one that is twelve feet wide. The wider raft will be able to carry more people standing on the edge without tipping over than the narrower one. As the weighted side sinks, the other side lifts out of the water, so the wider it is the more there is to be lifted out of the water. We should point out, however, the difference between "initial" and "ultimate" stability.

A flat raft has high "initial stability" because it takes a lot of weight to tip it just a little bit. But the deeper the weighted side sinks into the water the less additional weight is needed to sink it further. It will tip over very easily after it gets to a steep angle and thus has very poor "ultimate stability." A deep, narrow boat with a heavy keel may tip the first few degrees very easily, but as the keel gets lifted higher and higher by the heel angle, the more effective it becomes. So the deep keelboat may have poor "initial stability" but excellent "ultimate stability."

Stability is essentially controlled by the relationship of the position of the Center of Gravity (CG) of the boat to that of the Center of Buoyancy (CB) of the boat. The boat's CG is the center of the earth's gravitational pull on that particular boat. If the boat were suspended from a wire attached to its exact center of gravity, it could be rotated to any position and remain in that position when released. The Center of Buoyancy of the boat is really the center of gravity of all the water that the hull displaces. It is the center of all the buoyant forces pushing up on the hull. While the CG remains in one spot because the hull shape doesn't change, the CB moves in relation to what part of the hull is submerged. As the boat heels, one side submerges and the other side comes out of the water. The CB moves over further to the submerged side.

An interesting comparison results between the deep keelboat and the shallow beamy centerboarder. Figure 55A shows that at rest the CB and CG are usually in line one above another. (Crew weight plays a part in the position of the center of gravity, but we will disregard this for our purposes.) As the keelboat heels (Figure 55B) and CG moves to windward with the keel and the CB moves to leeward as the hull submerges. The greater distance the two move apart, the greater the lever-arm producing stability, with the gravitational forces pulling downward at the CG and the buoyant forces pushing upward at the CB. With the beamy centerboarder, the distance between the CG and CB is produced by the substantial lateral movement of the CB.

Figure 55C portrays the two boats flat on their sides, a rare occurrence. Note that the distance between the CB and CG of the keelboat is now the greatest it's been, whereas that of the centerboard boat has diminished. As a matter of fact, if the centerboarder tips a little further the CG will get on the other side of the CB and capsize the boat. If the keelboat tips further, it will turn right over (provided water can't get into the boat), turn turtle, and end up right side up again due to the lowness of the CG. This is called having "positive stability" -- the boat will always right itself.

Most cruising boats have self-draining cockpits, sliding hatches and hatch boards to ensure that water can't get into the boat if a freak wave flipped them over. The chances of a cruising boat turning over are slim indeed. There have been no more than two recorded incidents that I know of and one of them is doubtful. No boat is apt to turn turtle without losing it's mast due to the tremendous forces involved. One of the two indicated that the boat flipped, yet the mast was not lost, casting doubt upon the report's veracity.

Centerboarders, however, tend to capsize fairly easily so are usually limited in size to that which can be righted by the crew or at least with a minimum of outside assistance. There are some larger cruising boats that have centerboards. These boats are really keelboats in that they are self-righting (have positive stability) without use of the centerboard. The board is only used for balance and to reduce sideslipping (leeway) when sailing to windward.

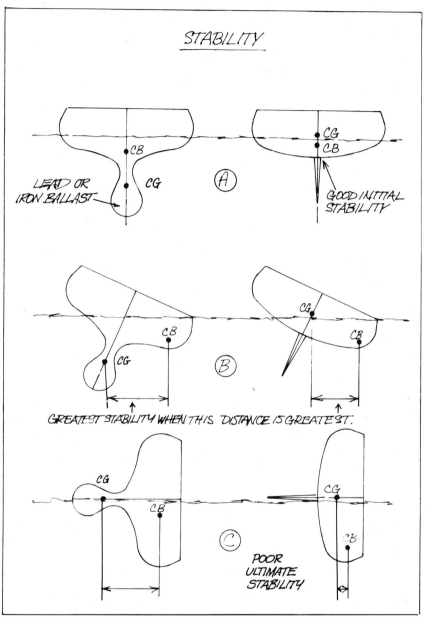

STABILITY

A

LEAD OR
IRON BALLAST

CB

CG

CG
CB

GOOD INITIAL
STABILITY

B

CG

CB

CG

CB

GREATEST STABILITY WHEN THIS DISTANCE IS GREATEST.

C

CG

CB

CG

CB

POOR
ULTIMATE
STABILITY

fig.55

HULL AND SAILS:
INTERRELATION IN BALANCE

Water flowing past the hull, keel and rudder of a sailboat is subject to the same basic rules as air flowing past the sails. The only difference between the sails and underwater appendages is that the latter are symmetrical while the former have the effect of being asymmetrical. But "angle of attack" (which we call "angle of incidence" for wind hitting the sails and "yaw angle" for water hitting the keel) solves the problem of getting "lift" from the keel.

Because of the pressure of the wind in the sails, a sailboat sideslips a little bit as it goes forward. This is called "making leeway." The angle between the direction that the boat is heading and an imaginary line indicating its "track" through the water is the "yaw angle" or "leeway angle" as shown in Figure 56A. Since the water has to travel a greater distance on the windward side of the keel, an area of reduced pressure results producing "lift" to windward. The more lift from the underwater surfaces, the less leeway the boat makes. In other words, it slips sideways less. Obviously, when sailing to windward we are trying to reach a destination upwind and any sideslipping that pushes us downwind is undesirable.

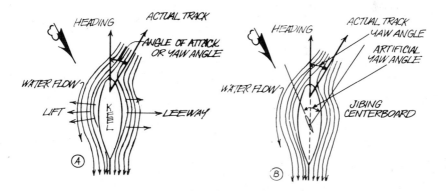

fig.56

The slower the velocity of the fluid flowing past the "airfoil" the less its efficiency as a lifting surface. So when the boat is going slowly, it sideslips more. This increases the leeway angle and, up to a point, increases the efficiency of the keel. Past that point, though, the water becomes turbulent on the windward side of the keel and a stall results. A good example of this situation is a sailboat sitting on the starting line before a race in a closehauled pointing angle but with sails luffing, waiting for the starting gun. At the gun, the crew trims in the sails to get the boat moving forward. Instead, the boat goes almost as fast sideways as she goes forward because the velocity of the water flowing past the keel is not sufficient to counteract the sideways push of the sails. The helmsman would better have sailed on a slight reach where the force of the sails is more in the direction of the boat's heading in order to pick up speed and then harden up to closehauled.

Many boats have what are called "jibing" centerboards (Figure 56B). This means that they can be angled towards the wind to produce an artificial yaw angle. The idea is to set the centerboard as if the boat were side-slipping in order to make a larger angle of attack to the water and reduce leeway. An added advantage is that the hull, which creates a great deal of drag if going sideways through the water, is headed more in the direction of the boat's track. Only the centerboard, the effective lifting surface, is cocked to windward. At high boat speeds, though, the skipper must be careful about cocking the centerboard too much because stalling will result. Just like the sail, where the airflow can't bend around a large curvature at high speed, the water is less able to bend around a centerboard with a large angle of attack the faster the boat sails.

The sails of a boat sailing upwind create a forward and sideways force. The keel or centerboard resists the sideways force. Unfortunately, due to drag, they also resist the forward force. But to get into that opens a whole Pandora's box of how to reduce "form" drag, "frictional" drag, and the hull's "wave-making" drag, which is really a subject for a book on naval architecture, not practical sailing.

Balance

In order to sail properly, and certainly to race successfully, one must take the "balance" of the boat in consideration. By "balance" we mean the tendency of the boat's heading to either deviate or to remain straight when the helmsman releases the tiller or wheel. If he lets go of the tiller and the boat turns away from the wind, to leeward, it is said to have "lee helm."

Conversely, if the boat turns to windward it has "weather helm." If it sails straight ahead, the boat is perfectly balanced.

Though the above can be used as a guideline, be careful not to be misled by "artificial" weather helm. A boat will normally turn into the wind when the tiller is released because of the forces acting on the rudder. As water flows past the windward side of a rudder, "lift" is generated due to the angle of attack with the water flow. If the rudder post (which turns the rudder) is located on the leading edge of the rudder and attached to the trailing edge of the keel, all the area aft of the post is pulling to windward, thus tending to turn the boat into the wind. Since the water flow has traveled the full length of the keel to reach the rudder, though, the flow is not very effective as a lift factor.

Separated or "spade" rudders have become increasingly popular on cruising boats recently. The rudder is placed near the stern of the boat where it has the greatest leverage for steering. It is a lifting surface in itself, and since it isn't attached to the keel and is meeting fairly non-turbulent water, such a rudder is very efficient. These rudders usually are "balanced" in that the rudder post enters the rudder about one-fourth of the way back rather than being attached along the leading edge. Hopefully then, the center of the pull to windward will be right at the post and the rudder will remain straight. This reduces artificial weather helm. It also decreases true weather helm because the rudder, as a lifting surface, pulls the stern of the boat to windward to a small extent.

Excessive leeway also causes artificial weather helm. Take an extreme example of a boat slipping straight sideways through the water and making no forward motion. The water on the leeward side of the rudder aft of the rudder post pushes the rudder to windward giving the appearance of weather helm.

The way one can distinguish the artificial from the true weather helm is if the rudder has to be deflected from straight ahead in order to make the boat sail straight. In other words, if the tiller is being held constantly a few degrees to windward to make the boat sail straight, there is a true weather helm.

I've sailed on cruising boats with balanced spade rudders that the owners swore sailed fastest with a "neutral" helm, and that once they developed a slight weather helm the boat slowed down. My observation was that though the helm felt neutral (there was no tug on it because the rudder post entered the rudder well aft of its leading edge) there was indeed a slight weather helm because the tiller was being held to windward a few degrees. When the weather helm developed to a point where the helmsman could feel it, the tiller was being held to windward at an angle large enough to increase rudder drag, thus slowing the boat down.

In most boats sailing to windward a little weather helm is desirable. Where the rudder is attached to the trailing edge of the keel, as in Figures 57A and B, it is obvious that the couple of degrees of rudder needed to counteract a slight weather helm tends to give the keel "lift" and reduce leeway. Too much weather helm, however, will just cause turbulence and drag as in Figure 57C.

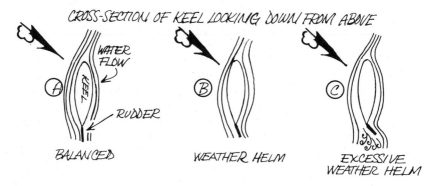

CROSS-SECTION OF KEEL LOOKING DOWN FROM ABOVE

A — WATER FLOW — KEEL — RUDDER — BALANCED

B — WEATHER HELM

C — EXCESSIVE WEATHER HELM

fig.57

The same holds true with the spade rudder, which gets its lift from the angle of attack the rudder makes with the water. A little weather helm cocks the rudder to windward and increases the angle of attack just like the "jibing centerboard" mentioned earlier.

There are many reasons for weather or lee helm, but foremost is the relationship between the "Center of Effort" of the sail plan and the "Center of Lateral Resistance" of the hull shape. Imagine a sailboat drifting sideways down a river with the current. It hangs up on a tree stump under the surface. At all locations *except one* on the underwater body of the boat it would pivot off the end of the stump and continue downstream. If it hangs up at that one spot, it will remain on the end of the stump in balance even with the current hitting the other side of the boat. This point is called the "Center of Lateral Resistance" of the boat, or CLR.

By geometrically determining the point that is the combined center of all the sails that are set on the boat, we can find the "Center of Effort," or CE of the boat. This is the center of all the forces acting to push the boat sideways against the center of all the forces resisting that push, the CLR.

Now imagine the boat as if it were a weather vane on top of a roof pivoting on the CLR. If the CE is directly above the CLR, the boat is in balance. So if the wind blows on this weather vane, it won't pivot.

However, by placing more sail area towards the bow of the boat, the CE moves forward. When it is forward of the CLR the tendency is for the bow of the boat to be blown to leeward. If you move the CE aft of the CLR by placing more sail area near the stern of the boat, the boat pivots to windward.

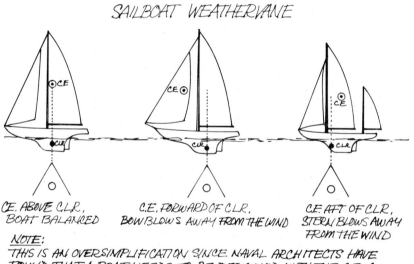

SAILBOAT WEATHERVANE

CE. ABOVE CLR,
BOAT BALANCED

C.E. FORWARD OF CLR.
BOW BLOWS AWAY FROM THE WIND

CE. AFT OF CLR,
STERN BLOWS AWAY
FROM THE WIND

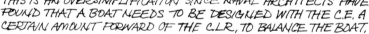

NOTE:
THIS IS AN OVERSIMPLIFICATION SINCE NAVAL ARCHITECTS HAVE FOUND THAT A BOAT NEEDS TO BE DESIGNED WITH THE C.E. A CERTAIN AMOUNT FORWARD OF THE C.LR., TO BALANCE THE BOAT,

fig.58

The easiest way, in theory, to change the balance of a boat would be to move the sail area forward or aft. If you move the mast (and along with it, the main and jib) aft, you increase weather helm, and if you move the rig forward you reduce weather helm or increase lee helm. Since most boats have varying amounts of weather helm and rarely have lee helm, any change that results in lee helm is usually just a reduction in weather helm for most boats and we tend to state it that way.

In practice, moving the whole rig fore and aft can be time consuming on a small boat and well-nigh impossible on a large one without extensive carpentry. A solution is to change the amount of sail forward or aft. A friend of mine had a yawl which never seemed to develop any weather helm, so he replaced the mizzen mast with a larger one, bought a new mizzen and at long last achieved weather helm. Another friend owns a sloop that constantly developed too much weather helm. When nothing else seemed to work, he put a bowsprit on the boat and bought a larger genoa with the desired results. The former brought the CE aft to achieve weather helm, while the latter brought the CE forward to reduce it.

Obviously, if changing the amount of sail area fore or aft changes the balance of the boat, changing the efficiency of the sails will have the same effect. If you sail without a jib your boat will have a strong weather helm from the mainsail and if you sail under jib alone the boat will have a strong lee helm. If you luff the mainsail, thereby reducing its efficiency, the CE moves forward with a corresponding reduction of weather helm. If you luff the jib, you will increase weather helm.

By careful adjustment of the main and jib we can steer a fairly accurate course without even touching the tiller. This is good practice because one never knows when a rudder might fall off or a tiller break. One time we lost a rudder in the middle of a Transatlantic Race and steered the last 1000 miles by adjusting the sails alone. For a closehauled course, trim the jib fairly flat and then play the mainsheet -- luffing the main to head off and trimming it to head up.

On a small boat the distribution of your crew weight will have an effect on balance. When a boat heels the bow wave on the lee side becomes larger (Figure 59) and tends to shove the bow to windward.

fig.59

Also, the center of effort (CE) is out over the water (Figures 60A and 60B). Imagine a sailboat in a dead flat calm with the mainsail and boom way out over the water as if it were running free. If you come along in an outboard motorboat and push the end of the boom in the direction that the boat is pointing, the boat will turn away from you (into the imaginary wind). The reason, of course, is that the push is out on a lever arm, at the other end of which is the drag of the hull. So, you can see that *additional* weather helm develops when the center of effort is out over the water when you are reaching, running or heeling.

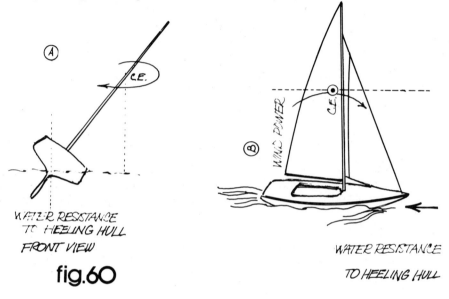

WATER RESISTANCE
TO HEELING HULL
FRONT VIEW

fig.60

WATER RESISTANCE
TO HEELING HULL

By shifting the crew weight from one side of the boat to the other, a small sailboat can be steered without using the rudder if the breeze is light enough.

The center of effort can be moved in a few other more subtle ways. If a mast is raked aft the sail area is moved aft. Raking a mast means leaning it, and is not to be confused with bending it. To lean it aft, the headstay is eased and the backstay is tightened.

Sail shape also has a great deal of effect on balance. For instance, if the mainsail has a tight leech (one in which the batten ends are pulled slightly inboard, to windward) weather helm will be increased.

Another way to change the balance of the boat is to leave the center of effort in one place and move the center of lateral resistance forward or aft. Since the CLR is the center of the underwater lateral plane of the boat, the only way (without a centerboard) to move it is to submerse less or more of the boat. If you depress the bow of the boat by moving crew or equipment forward, the CLR moves forward and weather helm increases. The opposite results if you depress the stern, allowing the bow to lift higher out of the water. Imagine the bow being blown to leeward by the wind as more of it is exposed. This is only a memory aid and not the cause of the lee helm.

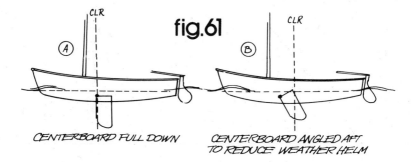

CENTERBOARD FULL DOWN   CENTERBOARD ANGLED AFT
                             TO REDUCE WEATHER HELM

Sailboats that have centerboards can move the CLR more easily. Since a centerboard pivots on a forward pin it describes an arc as it is lowered. Thus the area is further aft when the board is halfway down (angled aft) than in its full down position (vertical under the pin). So to move the CLR aft, just raise the board partway if it's all the way down or lower it partway if it's fully housed in the centerboard trunk (all the way up). This will have the effect of reducing weather helm.

A well designed boat will have a slight weather helm which increases as the wind velocity increases. The weather helm creates "lift" for the rudder, and also gives the helmsman some "feel" for the boat. The slight tug allows the helmsman to ease his pressure on the tiller in order to let the boat come up closer to the wind. He increases his pressure on the tiller to get the boat to fall off away from the wind. In other words, he is steering only one direction, while the boat steers itself the other direction. A boat is very difficult to steer well if it has to be steered up towards the wind as well as away from the wind. It is said to have no "feel."

Another reason it is desirable to have some weather helm is the fact that with weather helm the boat will automatically head up in the puffs. This reduces heeling and maintains the angle that the wind originally made with the sails, because the apparent wind comes aft in puffs. For the latter reason, even in light air, one should head up in the puffs.

To reduce excessive weather helm, you can (1) add more sail area forward, (2) reduce sail area or sail effectiveness aft, (3) move the mast forward, (4) reduce mast rake, (5) move crew or equipment aft, (6) reduce heeling by hiking or (7) place the centerboard in the halfway down position.

HULL SPEED

Generally, the larger the boat, the faster it can go. For a displacement boat, a heavy deep-keel boat, the maximum speed a given hull can attain from wind power is called "hull speed" and is largely dependent on the waterline length of the boat. Hull speed is expressed as $1.34\sqrt{LWL}$. If a cruising sailboat has a waterline length of 36 feet, she should be able to sail 1.34 x 6, or approximately eight knots.

The idea behind this is that a boat cannot travel faster than the wave she creates and the speed of a wave is $1.34\sqrt{\ell}$, "ℓ" being the distance between the crests. The length, "ℓ", of a wave increases proportionally as the height ("h") of the wave increases. So the higher the wave, the greater the distance between crests and the faster it travels. This relates to the sailboat in that as the sailboat's speed increases, the greater the volume of water the bow has to push aside and the larger the bow wave becomes. As the bow wave increases in height, the distance between its crest and that of the wave following it, the quarter wave, increases until it approaches the waterline length of the boat itself. This can be noted as the sailboat in Figures 62B and 62C picks up speed. At first there are numerous small "transverse" waves while the boat travels slowly. These spread out as the bow wave increases in height until, in Figure 62D, hull speed is attained and there are only two waves along the hull, the bow wave and the quarter wave. To push a boat past its theoretical hull speed, though possible, would take more power in wind and sails than most boats can withstand. A beautiful example of hull speed can be seen whenever a tugboat is cruising to a job. They have trememdous power and very easily reach hull speed. The classical wave pattern of a bow wave and quarter wave is always present at that speed. For a tugboat to go even marginally faster would take so much more power it would be uneconomical.

When a boat does exceed its hull speed, as the one being towed in Figure 62E, the stern tends to leave the quarter wave behind and drop into the trough between waves. The bow rides high in the air. Often one sees a number of displacement one-design racing sailboats being towed to a regatta at greater than hull speed. Their sterns are practically under the water.

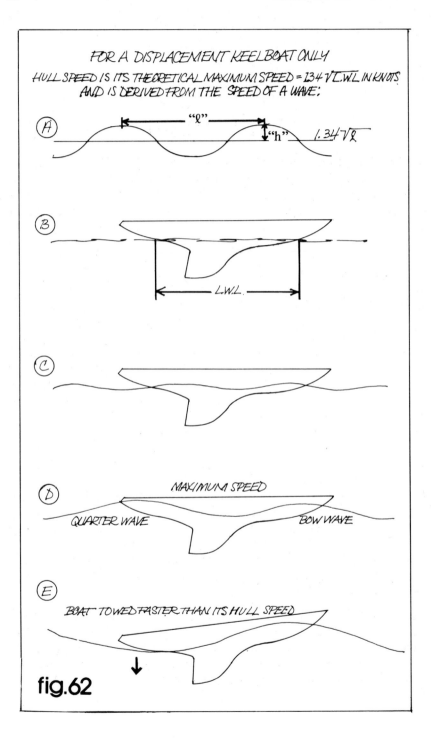

FOR A DISPLACEMENT KEELBOAT ONLY

HULL SPEED IS ITS THEORETICAL MAXIMUM SPEED = 1.34 √L.W.L. IN KNOTS
AND IS DERIVED FROM THE SPEED OF A WAVE:

(A)   "ℓ"   "h"   1.34 √ℓ

(B)   L.W.L.

(C)

(D)   MAXIMUM SPEED
      QUARTER WAVE   BOW WAVE

(E)   BOAT TOWED FASTER THAN ITS HULL SPEED

fig.62

Note that we keep reiterating "displacement" in reference to hull speed. The flat bottom centerboarder and many fin-keeled boats really don't have a hull speed. They are technically "planing" boats. A planing boat skims along the surface of the water like a skipping stone rather than plowing the water aside. Usually it has a v-shaped hull near the bow and a fairly flat bottom aft. As its speed increases the bow rides up on the bow wave and finally the boat levels off at planing speed with the bow wave well aft. Most powerboats, particularly in the 30 foot range, act this way. At lower speeds the boat plows through the water. Then as the speed increases and the bow wave moves aft, the bow rises up in the air. At a certain speed the unsupported bow, with the bow wave well aft, levels off as the boat breaks into a high speed plane. For a sailboat, its ability to plane or not depends on its length/weight ratio. If it's too heavy for its length it will never be able to plane.

There is a way that a displacement boat can exceed its theoretical hull speed, and that is by "surfing." Surfing is being pushed by a wave just the way surfers ride a wave on a surfboard. In large wave conditions, when running downwind, a sailboat can get on the front side of a wave and carry it for quite a number of seconds with a tremendous burst of speed. It takes good helmsmanship to be able to get on the wave just right to reap the greatest benefits from it. Though light planing boats tend to surf more easily, displacement boats are perfectly capable of surfing and can far exceed their hull speed in this manner.

RIGHT OF WAY

Power Versus Power

Quite often beginners feel that their sailboat always has right of way over powerboats even when running the engine. Not so. Only when a sailboat is not running its engine is it classified as a sailboat. So even if you have a day sailor with a tiny outboard motor, when the motor is running (even if the sails are set) you are liable to the motorboat "rules of the road" (as the right of way rules are called).

Though there are many minor ramifications, the main thing to remember when motorboats are on a converging collision course is that the one in the other's "danger zone" has the right of way. The "danger zone" of a motorboat is from dead ahead to two points abaft the starboard beam. If there is any boat approaching from that area you must avoid it. It is the "stand-on" vessel in that it has the right of way, and you are the "give-way" vessel in that you must keep clear. The obligation of the "stand-on" vessel is to hold its course and speed so you won't be misled in your attempt to keep clear. What must be avoided at all costs is the kind of mixup that occasionally happens to pedestrians going in opposite directions on a city street. One steps one way just as the other decides to pass on that side, then changes direction only to find the other changing the same way. On a boat this could bring about a serious collision, so the "stand-on" vessel *must* maintain her course until it is obvious that a collision is imminent, at which time she must avoid it.

If two boats are approaching each other from dead ahead, both should turn to starboard. If one is approaching the other from any point aft of the danger zone, he is overtaking and must keep clear of the overtaken boat.

Power Versus Sail

The above should be enough basic information to keep you out of trouble when you are running your engine and meet another powerboat. Another set of rules applies when you are sailing and meet a power boat. Many people have the misconception that a sailboat always has right of way over a motorboat. Though this is usually true there are a number of exceptions when a sailboat doesn't have rights: When the motorboat is anchored or disabled, is being overtaken by the sailboat or, when the motorboat is a commercial vessel with limited maneuverability in a narrow channel.

Sail Versus Sail

There are only three basic possibilities when your sailboat approaches another: (1) You are on the same tack as the other boat, (2) you are on opposite tacks or (3) one of the boats is overtaking the other.

For this reason there are three basic rules to cover the three possibilities: (1) On the same tack, the leeward boat has right of way, (2) on opposite tacks, the starboard tack boat has right of way and (3) if overtaking, the boat ahead (the overtaken boat) has right of way.

There are three sets of general rules used by United States yachtsmen: the International Rules, the Inland Rules and the Racing Rules. The International Rules and the Inland Rules agree with each other practically verbatim.

The Racing Rules agree with the three basic International and Inland Rules with one exception: the overtaking rule is in effect, but the opposite tack rule overrides it if the situation arised. For example, (1) a port tack boat keeps clear of another port tack boat it is overtaking, (2) a port tack boat keeps clear of a starboard tack boat it is overtaking, but (3) a starboard tack boat doesn't have to keep clear of a port tack boat it is overtaking. This could only occur on a dead run and the defense for the port tack boat is to flip over to the starboard tack.

TEST QUESTIONS -- SECTION THREE

1. Describe positive stability.
2. What is yaw angle?
3. What is a balanced rudder?
4. Why is excessive weather helm detrimental?
5. How do you reduce weather helm?
6. How do you steer without a rudder?
7. Define Center of Effort.
8. Define Center of Lateral Resistance.
9. Describe hull speed.
10. Describe planing.
11. Describe surfing.
12. In the following situations, determine which boat has the right of way under each rule—International/Inland and Racing.

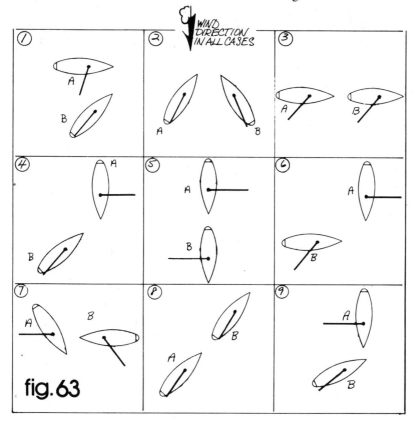

fig. 63

HEAVY WEATHER

Though we advise beginners to sail only on pleasant days, after you have gained some confidence in your abilities try sailing on progressively windier days.

I know an owner of a cruising boat who races. Every spring he picks the windiest day he can find to go out and practice. The result is that he gains complete confidence in his boat, equipment and crew. If you can handle so much wind, any less windy day is a breeze (pardon the pun).

Until you either sail in a great deal of wind or get caught out in a passing squall you won't have confidence in your ability to handle the boat in a heavy wind situation. The best way to put your mind at rest is to imagine the worst that can happen -- capsizing, man overboard or loss of the mast. None of these three is so frightening. If you are sailing a centerboarder, practice capsizing and righting the boat. After capsizing, swim the bow of the boat around into the wind so the wind can get under the sails and separate them from the water as the boat comes up. Then stand on the centerboard to apply righting leverage to the boat, scramble in when it's upright and bail it out or sail it dry if it has venturi bailers or transom flaps.

Practice man overboard by tossing out a cushion and seeing how fast you can retrieve it, making sure to bring the boat to a complete stop.

You can't practice loss of the mast, but you can be prepared for that eventuality. An anchor with plenty of line, a paddle and a first-aid kit would help put your mind at ease. On a larger boat, wire cutters would be a good idea for cutting away a mast that might be damaging the hull.

Once you are confident that there is nothing that could happen to you or the boat that you can't handle, then all the rest is just sound and fury. It's natural to be a bit apprehensive or frightened of heavy winds at first, but soon you'll find that you actually enjoy the heavy stuff -- an exciting part of sailing!

When you get caught in your first squall remember that the most important thing to do is shorten sail. You may see the squall approaching and get some sail down before it hits if it looks bad enough, though it's hard to judge without a great deal of experience just how bad a squall will be. Sometimes a nasty looking sky turns out to be only dark clouds and rain, but no more wind. However, when a bad squall hits, the wind can go from 10 mph to 40 or 50 mph in seconds. If you hadn't reduced sail previously, you should have at least prepared for the possibility of having to. Halyards should be neatly coiled and ready to run. Each crew member should be briefed as to what his responsibilities will be if the squall is a bad one so not a second is lost in giving orders. This has a secondary advantage of decreasing the chance of panic. When the first blast hits and the boat is laid over on its side, the brain processes of even some experienced crew members tend to become stupefied. If he knows what he is expected to do beforehand, he doesn't have to think.

On a small boat, the mainsail usually has greater sail area than the jib and should be the first sail to lower. If it isn't lowered, as the wind increases the skipper should release the mainsheet to reduce heeling. The boat, due to the weight of the wind and sea, will probably be on more of a close reach than closehauled. At some point, even with the main and jib luffing completely, the wind force will be sufficient to lay the boat over on its side. The boom and mainsail will hit the water to leeward which, due to the boat's forward motion, will force the sail in towards the center of the boat just at a time when you want to let it out. The drag on the end of the boom pivots the boat to leeward just when you want to head up into the wind. The mainsail fills and over you go if it's a capsizable boat. So lower the mainsail first! The boat should sail well under jib alone.

If it's still blowing too hard, lower all sails and run before the wind "under bare poles" (no sail), unless there's a chance of running aground.

Your best friend in bad conditions may very well be your anchor. If the visibility is down to a few feet, you're not sure of your position and you're afraid you may be blown ashore, get your anchor over the side. You may not have enough line to reach bottom, but you can be fairly sure that the anchor will hook before you get into water shallow enough for your boat to go aground, or be swamped by breakers.

On a cruising boat, the genoa often has much more sail area than the main. If you're caught with the genoa up in a squall, that's the sail you should lower. The cruising boat has better stability than the small centerboarder, so there is no need to worry about dipping the main boom. The boat should sail well under main alone until you can put on a storm jib, and the main can usually be reefed if necessary.

ANCHORING

After you've learned to sail, it probably won't be long before you do some cruising. You'll sail along some coast putting into little harbors at night. When choosing a spot to anchor make sure it's in sheltered water, not in a channel, and check the chart to determine that there's enough water for your boat in that location at low tide. Then choose a spot with enough room to swing around your anchor without hitting other anchored boats. Boats of the same type will swing about the same way. For instance, a deep-keeled sailboat will line up more with the current while a shallow draft powerboat with high superstructure will line up more with the wind. Drive past a harbor and sometimes you will see the sailboats pointing in one direction and the powerboats in another. So, if you anchor among other boats, make sure you are closer to the ones that are similar to yours.

Next get the anchor out on deck, coil the anchor line so it will run free, and secure the bitter end. Many anchors have been lost because the end hasn't been tied and the man feeding out the line gets to the end before he expects to. It can happen easily at night when, because of an increase in wind velocity, a crew member lets out more line to improve the holding power of the anchor and doesn't realize the end wasn't tied until it's too late.

Allow the boat to coast to a complete stop at the point where you want to be and toss the anchor over the side making sure the line doesn't get tangled in the flukes as it goes. It's supposed to be bad practice to toss the anchor rather than lower it over the side, but everybody does it and as long as the anchor is light and you're careful to avoid the line tangling it isn't all that bad. As the boat starts to drift backwards, feed out line until about 5 to 1 "scope" is attained. This means you have let out five times as much line as the depth of the water. If the water were 20 feet deep, you would have let out about 100 feet of line. A scope of four or five to one should be adequate in most cases where the bottom is good for holding and there's not much wind or you're anchoring for a short time. Increase the scope if there's a lot of wind or you want to be sure you won't drag. The smaller the angle the anchor line makes with the bottom, the greater the holding power of the anchor because the line will be pulling the anchor along the bottom rather than lifting it off the bottom. When you feel you have eased out sufficient scope, snub the anchor line around a cleat so that the momentum of the boat will jerk the anchor home much like one jerks a fishing line to sink the hook into the fish's mouth. Check that you're not dragging by pulling on the line and, from time to time, by glancing at your relationship with points on shore and with other boats.

The next morning when you want to leave, reverse the process. If you have an engine, power along the anchor line towards the anchor with the man in the bow overhauling (gathering in) the slack line. When the bow of the boat is directly above the anchor, again snub the line on a cleat and let the momentum of the boat break the anchor free. If the anchor is still stuck, give your boat a little more power and try pulling from different directions in hopes of rotating the anchor. Remember that sailboats have powerful winches that can be used as an aid. Also, if the seas are heavy, as the bow goes down take in any slack in the anchor line and snub it. Then, as the bow rises on the next wave, the buoyancy of the boat may break free the anchor. To be successful with this method, you will probably have to take in the slack on a number of waves before you have it all.

DOCKING

Under sail, docking isn't much different from picking up a man overboard or a mooring. The boat has to be headed into the wind to stop. If the wind direction is parallel to the dock, (Figure 64A) just shoot the boat into the wind and come to a stop parallel to and alongside the dock. If the wind is blowing away from the dock and towards the water (Figure 64B), shooting into the wind takes you straight into the dock. If you're going too fast remember you can back your main to slow down. Approaching at an angle would be better than approaching head on. Avoid coming in perfectly parallel to the dock if the wind is blowing out from it, because when you luff the sails to slow down you will start drifting sideways away from the dock, unless it's a long one and a crew member can hop onto the dock with a line before the boat slows down too much.

If the wind is blowing perpendicular to the dock and towards it from the water, docking is more difficult. The best approach is without any sail up if the wind is heavy or with only the jib if the wind is light. So round up into the wind to windward of the dock as in Figure 64C and lower the sails. Then drift into the dock. You'd be surprised how well some boats can sail without any sail up. A Soling, for instance, will sail practically on a beam reach without sail once it has picked up some speed.

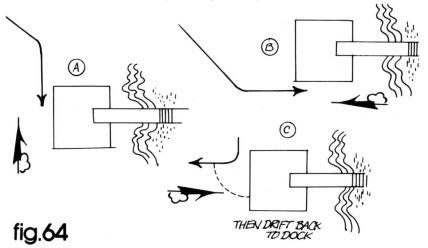

THEN DRIFT BACK
TO DOCK

fig.64

99

If you have a cruising sailboat you will probably power into the dock. Generally, the same rules apply as with sail but you have more flexibility. If possible, approach the dock upwind and/or upcurrent depending on the force of each. The one most common mistake is approaching too fast. The cruising sailboat has a great deal of momentum and is hard to stop. It usually has a small two-bladed propeller hidden behind the keel. The result is that you can put the engine in reverse, rev it up and the boat still moves forward, gradually slowing down. I knew a man who had a beautiful 48-foot sailboat with a Mercedes diesel as auxiliary power. He always approached the dock too fast. About 100 yards away he'd be going five knots, put the engine in reverse and hope that the boat would come to a stop by the time it was alongside. One day, when there was a 60-foot yacht on the far end of the dock, sticking out at right angles to the long side that my friend planned to approach, he misjudged the speed. Even though the engine was screaming in reverse we were now alongside the dock with about two knots of headway and heading straight for the bow section of the other yacht extending past the edge of the dock end. My friend couldn't steer out because the stern would just bump if he tried to make such a sharp turn. Luckily I was able to toss a bow line to the other boat's owner who ran aft and snubbed it around a piling. Our bow crunched into the dock as the boat's forward motion was checked just short of a collision.

A line tied aft from the bow is one of the common lines used in tying a boat up at a dock. It's called a "forward spring" line and keeps the boat from moving forward. An "after spring" line runs from the stern to a point forward on the dock and keeps the boat from drifting backwards. These spring lines combine with the bow and stern lines to keep the boat parallel to the dock so it will rest on fenders and not rub its topsides on the dock or on pilings.

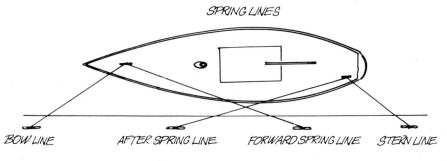

SPRING LINES

BOW LINE   AFTER SPRING LINE   FORWARD SPRING LINE   STERN LINE

fig.64 d

NAVIGATION

It's not our purpose here to delve very deeply into coastal navigation or "piloting" as it is commonly called. We just want you to be able to plot a course that avoids hazards.

Compass Variation

Our chief navigational aid is the compass. There are various errors one must be aware of. First the compass does not point to the North Pole (true north) but rather to a magnetic mass (magnetic north). The difference between the direction the compass is pointing and true north is called *Variation.* It changes according to geographical location, as shown on your chart. Printed on the chart is a "compass rose." North on the outer rose is true, while north on the inner rose is magnetic. Since the inner rose already has taken variation into account, as long as we use the inner rose for plotting our courses, we can forget about having to compute variation. Since we are using a magnetic compass, magnetic directions are all we care about and can be taken right off the chart. There's no reason to get a true course first and then convert to magnetic by applying variation, though this over-complicated process is still used by many people.

Compass Deviation

Deviation is a more subtle form of compass error. Magnetic portions of the boat itself tend to affect the compass. On a sailboat, though, after the compass has been checked and adjusted, deviation rarely amounts to more than one degree. Since you can't steer anywhere near that close, it's not worth worrying about. Again, just be aware that deviation exists. If you want to check your compass to make sure that the compass isn't way off, pick two points such as landmarks or buoys (though the latter are not as accurate as a lighthouse), compute the course between these points on a chart, and run between them. The course shown on your compass should be the same as the one you computed. Run in four directions, north, south, east and west, because the deviation could be small going north and large going the opposite direction. You will probably find that on a sailboat the error is negligible particularly if you are sailing on a small body of water with relatively short distances between the buoys you'd be using for navigation. A five degree error in heading for a course between two buoys a mile apart means you can still practically touch the second buoy when you come abeam or it. However, if you were steering a course for twenty miles, the five degree error would make a substantial difference on your final location. Don't let me lull you into carelessness, though. Accuracy is a habit one should foster when navigating. You never know when you'll be caught in a dense fog and need all the accuracy you can muster.

Chart Distances

The vertical chart lines are *meridians,* or "degrees of longitude" which point to the North and South Poles on a globe, but are parallel when spread out on the "Mercator projection" (the one we use for most of our coastal navigation). The horizontal lines are *parallels,* "degrees of latitude." There are sixty minutes to a degree; thus each minute of latitude (and longitude, at the equator) equals one nautical mile. To measure distance we can use the gradations along the side edges of the chart. In many cases each mile so shown is divided into tenths for accuracy and ease in measuring distance. If you want to know how far it is between two buoys, place one point of a set of dividers on one buoy and spread them so that the other point is on the other buoy. Then move them to the edge of the chart and see how many minutes fall within the points. If the distance was seven minutes, that converts to seven nautical miles. If you are traveling 3.5 knots (a knot is one nautical mile in one hour so never say "3.5 knots per hour" because that's like saying "3.5 miles per hour per hour") then you will cover that distance in two hours.

Plotting a Course

When we draw a course line on a chart, we want to know the magnetic direction of the line because it represents our boat moving on a compass course. The compass rose on the chart represents the boat's compass pointing to magnetic north. What we'd like to do is move the compass rose over, place it on our course line and read our course off it as if it were the boat's compass. Since the rose is printed on the chart, we can't do it that way, so we have to do the next best thing -- move the course line over to the compass rose. To accomplish this we use an instrument called a "parallel ruler" or "parallel rules," a dandy nautical gadget for carrying a line from one chart position to another, exactly parallel to the original line so that its direction will remain the same.

Lay the edge of your parallel rulers along the desired course. Press down on one leg and move the other out in the direction of the nearest compass rose. Then press that one down and move the first in parallel. Alternately, press-spread, press-spread the legs of the ruler until you have centered one edge of the parallel ruler right over the cross in the center of the compass rose. Then read, under the magnetic rose, the course in degrees.

Four mistakes are commonly made by beginners: (1) letting the parallel rulers slip so that they are no longer parallel to the course line, (2) reading the course off the outside (true) rose rather than the inside (magnetic) one, (3) reading the wrong increment (the smaller roses have increments of two degrees while on the larger ones every degree is marked) and (4) reading off the wrong edge of the circle -- in other words, reading 270 degrees (west) when you're actually traveling 90 degrees (east).

Chart Reading

Buoys are marked on the chart as small diamonds with a dot underneath to indicate their exact location. The color of the diamond, usually red or black, corresponds to the color of the buoy. The most common ones are "nuns" and "cans." Nuns are red, conical and even numbered. Cans are black, cylindrical and odd numbered. Next to the diamond on the chart will be, for example, N"4", so you know that it's a nun with the number "4" painted on it. Or it might read C"3" to indicate a can buoy painted with the number "3".

If the dot under the diamond is in the center of a small purplish circle it means the buoy is lighted. The characteristics of the light are written alongside. "Fl R 3 sec" means it's a flashing red light going on every three seconds. "FG" would mean "fixed green." A note such as "60 FT 13 M" would mean that the light is sixty feet above the surface of the water and has a visibility of 13 miles.

Study a chart and familiarize yourself with the various other abbreviations. The colors on a chart are important. White areas are deep water, light blue is under 20 feet deep and green is out of the water at low tide. Check how the depth is indicated. On most U.S. charts the depths are in feet at mean low water. Also, there are contour lines at certain constant depths, so you can get the idea of the bottom contour.

Remember the time-honored navigational byword: "Red...Right...Returning," which means that red buoys are left to starboard when entering a harbor or when sailing from a larger body of water into a smaller one.

Bearings

Navigation on a sailboat is slightly complicated by the fact that we can't always steer the course we want -- if our destination is dead upwind, for example. On a powerboat we could plot all our courses the night before and run the preset courses allowing for current and drift. But with a sailboat we are mainly keeping track of our location as we sail along and adjusting our course to the desired destination accordingly.

One of the best methods of determining your position is by taking bearings. Sight over your compass at two or three lights or landmarks and record your bearing to each in degrees. For each one, locate the same number on the nearest magnetic rose (inner circle) on the chart. Place an outside edge of your parallel rules on both this number and the cross in the very center of the rose. Work the other outside edge of the parallel rules along the chart to the landmark (that you took the bearing on) and draw a line through it -- extending the line out into the water. You are located somewhere along this line. Now repeat the process using the bearings you had for the second and third landmarks or lights. Taking three bearings will give you a triangle when plotted, which is a bit more accurate than the cross you get from only two bearings. If the triangle is too large you should take your bearings again because one was probably inaccurate. Ideally, you would want all three to cross at exactly one point -- your position -- but that rarely happens.

When you choose the lights or landmarks, try to pick ones that are quite a distance from each other. If you are using only two bearings your greatest accuracy would be from two that were 90 degrees apart from your position. Figure 65 shows bearings taken with a 5 degree error in each. Note that using landmarks A and B produces a much larger aggregate error than using A and C which are farther apart.

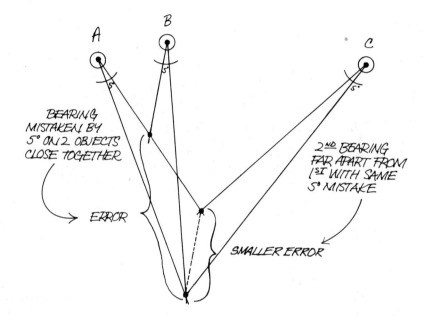

BEARING
MISTAKEN BY
5° ON 2 OBJECTS
CLOSE TOGETHER

2ND BEARING
FAR APART FROM
1ST WITH SAME
5° MISTAKE

ERROR

SMALLER ERROR

fig.65

458
458

EX 64

Photo by Walter Iooss, Courtesy of Sports Illustra

SPINNAKER

We will conclude these lessons with a fast basic rundown of spinnaker work, for those beginners, and there are always a few, who instinctively master the essentials of sailing early, and thirst for the delight (and extra work) of sailing under this most picturesque of sails.

The spinnaker is like a large parachute that pulls the boat downwind. It can be set with the true wind direction anywhere from dead astern to about abeam. It's made of light nylon and adds so much sail area to the total sail plan of the boat that speed is markedly increased when a spinnaker is set.

Refer to Figure 66 and learn the various lines involved with spinnaker work. The spinnaker is hoisted by the spinnaker halyard. One corner is held in place by the spinnaker pole which is always set to windward opposite the main boom. The corner attached to the pole is the tack of the spinnaker and attached to it is the spinnaker "after guy" or more commonly, "guy." The free corner of the spinnaker has a sheet attached to it like any other sail. The only tricky thing about the foregoing terminology is that during a jibe, the pole is switched over to the new windward side and the old guy becomes the new sheet (attached to the free corner of the sail) and the old sheet becomes the new guy (running through the jaws in the end of the pole).

There are two lines to hold the pole in position -- the topping lift to keep it from falling when the spinnaker isn't full of wind, and the foreguy (some people call it the spinnaker pole downhaul) to keep the pole from "skying" (pointing way up in the air) when the spinnaker is full.

TYPICAL SPINNAKER RIG

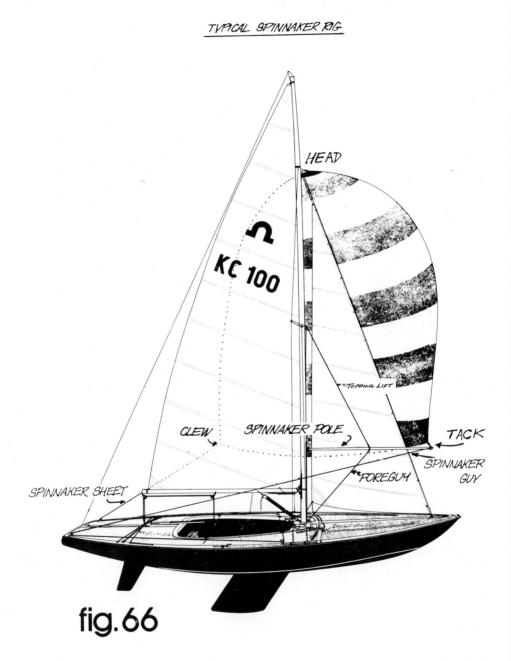

fig.66

Preparation for Setting the Spinnaker

Starting at the head of the spinnaker, run down both edges one at a time folding each accordion-style, holding the folds in one hand as you go. This will ensure that the spinnaker isn't twisted. If two edges are untwisted the third one, the foot in this case, also has to be straight.

Then, holding onto the folded edges and all three corners of the sail, stuff it into whatever container the boat uses to set the spinnaker from. This used to be called a "turtle" because it was originally a plywood board covered with black inner tube rubber with an opening at one end. When the spinnaker was stuffed in it, with the three corners hanging out the open end, and placed on the foredeck of the boat near the bow, it looked like a turtle. This term has been carried over even though spinnakers are now stuffed into bags, buckets or even cardboard boxes.

The halyard, sheet and guy are then connected to the three corners. Make sure the halyard is attached to the head of the sail -- the corner with the swivel. Since the spinnaker is vertically symmetrical, you can attach the sheet and guy to either of the other two corners. Make sure the sheet and guy are outside of everything on the boat (shrouds, stays, etc.) before connecting them.

In the case of a Soling or larger boat, the spinnaker is usually set on the leeward side. In smaller boats, where there is danger of capsizing if a crew member goes to the leeward side of the boat, the spinnaker is set to windward and pulled around the jibstay.

Next, set up the pole to windward with the guy running through the outboard end.

The Hoist

The key to a good set is to separate the lower corners of the spinnaker as the halyard is being raised. Often this means cleating the sheet and pulling the tack of the sail out to the pole as quickly as possible with the guy, unless you have enough crew to have a man on the sheet also. The halyard should be pulled up smartly so the spinnaker will neither fall overboard in the water nor will fill with air before it's all the way up. If the latter happens the halyard man may have difficulty holding on unless he gets a wrap around a winch or cleat in a hurry.

The Set

There are a few simple rules that form a good foundation for basic spinnaker work: (1) Set the pole at right angles to the apparent wind. Use the masthead fly since it's in less disturbed air than the shroud telltales and make sure the pole lies perpendicular to it.

(2) Since the spinnaker is a symmetrical sail, it should look symmetrical. Neither corner should be higher than the other. If the clew is higher than the tack, the pole should be raised to even them out.

(3) The pole should be perpendicular to the mast so it will hold the tack of the spinnaker as far away from the blanketing effect of the mainsail as possible. If the pole needs to be raised, as in rule #2, don't just pull the topping lift (which raises only the outboard end), but raise the inboard end also if it's adjustable.

(4) Ease the sheet until a curl appears along the luff of the "chute" (short for parachute spinnaker, as it was formerly called) and then trim it back until the curl disappears. The spinnaker trimmer will have to watch the luff of the spinnaker constantly, because the moment he looks away the chute will collapse, almost as if it were waiting for him to look away.

If you follow these few basic rules you shouldn't have any trouble learning to fly a spinnaker.

The Jibe

There are two basic types of jibes: the "end for end" jibe used on small boats with light spinnaker poles and the "dip-pole" jibe used on larger boats when the pole is heavy.

We'll concern ourselves with the former since it is applicable to the type of boat most learn on. The man on the foredeck stands behind the pole facing forward. Just before the jibe he disconnects the pole end from the mast and, as the boat turns downwind, he grabs the sheet and snaps the jaw of the pole over it. Then he passes the pole across the boat, unsnaps the other end from the old guy and snaps it into the eye on the mast. Meanwhile, the man in the cockpit is easing the sheet and trimming the guy as the boat turns into a jibe. This keeps the spinnaker downwind and full of air. The skipper pulls the main across and, if it is blowing hard, after the boom crosses the centerline, he turns the boat back downwind to keep it from broaching (rounding up broadside to the wind) which it has a tendency to do after a jibe.

The Douse

Taking a spinnaker down is much like running a movie of the hoist backwards. First grab the sheet as near the clew as possible and pull it into the cockpit so the spinnaker will come down behind the mainsail. Second, let the guy run free and start gathering in the foot of the sail. Third, lower the halyard fairly fast, but not so fast that you get ahead of the man gathering it in lest the sail falls in the water.

TEST QUESTIONS -- SECTION FOUR

1. On a small boat, which sail do you lower first in a squall?
2. Define scope.
3. Name some ways to raise a stuck anchor?
4. Describe spring lines.
5. Describe variation.
6. Describe deviation.
7. What distance is represented by two minutes of latitude?
8. What are four common mistakes made in plotting a course?
9. What does "Red Right Returning" mean?
10. List the steps involved in the spinnaker hoist, set and douse.

APPENDIX I

SAILING CHECKLIST

1. When boarding, step in the middle of the boat (on floorboards, not on the seat), holding onto the shrouds if possible and immediately lower the centerboard, if there is one.

2. Hank on the jib, tack first, feeding it between your legs for control.

3. Check along the foot for twists. Reave and attach the jib sheets. Tie stop knot in end. Attach jib halyard after checking for twists.

4. Feed the foot of the mainsail along the boom. Attach the tack, the clew, then pull the foot tight with the clew outhaul.

5. Put the battens in the batten pockets, starting with the lowest, with the most flexible ones highest up, thin end in first, hole end in last.

6. Follow along the luff to remove twists and feed the luff onto the mast starting at the head. Attach main halyard.

7. Attach rudder and tiller, if necessary.

8. Make sure the mainsheet is completely free to run, check halyard for twists, raise the main.

9. Take out the boom crutch (if any) as the main is being raised and hold the boom up by hand.

10. Make sure the leech of the main isn't caught under a spreader as the sail is raised.

11. Secure and coil the main halyard. You can use a half-hitch here, but not on sheets.

12. Pull the main downhaul tight if there is one.

13. Raise and secure the jib.

14. Untie the mooring line, but hold onto it. Back the jib to the desired tack and drop the mooring.

15. Don't cleat the mainsheet on a small boat in a breeze.

16. When checking the sail trim, adjust the jib first. Ease it until it luffs, then trim it in. Next, do the same with the main.

17. For extra speed raise the centerboard when on a run. When jibing have it partway down. To windward on a breezy day have it partway up to reduce weather helm.

18. Man overboard -- PRACTICE THIS!
    a)   Toss life preserver or floating cushion to him.
    b)   If closehauled or on a reach, jibe and shoot into the wind alongside the man.
    c)   If on a run, harden up to closehauled, tack, and shoot for him.

19. Capsize:
    a)   STAY WITH THE BOAT until help arrives! DON'T try to swim for shore.
    b)   Try to lower the sails, so righting the boat will be easier.
    c)   If the boat is small enough, point the bow to the wind and stand on the centerboard to right it.

APPENDIX II

PARTS OF THE BOAT

1. Port and Starboard Side -- Facing toward the bow of the boat, the port side is on your left and the starboard side is on your right.

2. *Beam* -- The widest part of the boat.

3. *Length Overall* -- The length of the hull between extremities (not including bowsprit).

4. *Waterline Length* -- The straight-line distance between the point where the bow emerges from the water and the point where the stern emerges from the water.

5. *Draft* -- The distance from the waterline to the lowest part of the boat.

6. *Topsides* -- The sides of the boat between the waterline and the deck.

7. *Aft* -- Near the stern, behind, in back.

8. *Tiller* -- A stick attached to the rudder for steering.

9. *Rudder* -- A flat, hinged board near the stern that deflects the passing water one way or the other to change the boat's direction.

10. *Cockpit* -- The part of the boat that is not decked over.

11. *Standing Rigging* -- All the permanent wires that hold the mast up. Broken down into two categories:
    a. *Stays* -- that keep the mast from falling toward the bow or stern.

b.   *Shrouds* -- that keep the mast from falling over the port or starboard side (upper and lower shrouds).

12. *Running Rigging* -- All movable rigging mainly:

a.   *Halyards* -- The wires (and/or ropes) that pull the sails up. They are attached to the sails with *shackles* (u-shaped fittings).
Never -- let go of the end of a halyard. It will begin to swing in the breeze and slide its way up to the top of the mast.
Always -- make sure that both ends of a halyard are attached to something.

b.   *Sheets* -- The lines with which you trim the sails. The mainsheet is led through a series of *blocks* (pulleys) to your hand or a *cam cleat*. It controls the swing of the boom, in or out. The jibsheets are attached to the clew of the jib. They are led, one on either side of the mast, through the *fairleads* (eyes or blocks on a track), around a *winch* (cylindrical drum increasing your mechanical advantage) to your hand or cam cleat. The jib is almost always trimmed on the *leeward* side (where the boom is) of the boat. Stop knots should be tied in the end of the jibsheets.

13. Others:

Outhaul: The rope (and/or wire) that attaches the clew of the mainsail to the outboard end of the boom. It is used to adjust the tension along the foot of the mainsail. Taut, for a flat sail: sailing upwind and/or on a breezy day. Loose, for a baggy sail: sailing downwind and/or on a calm day.

Downhaul: The *tackle* (rope and blocks) that holds down the inboard end of the boom. It is used to adjust the tension along the luff of the mainsail. Just like the outhaul: taut, for a flat sail -- upwind and/or breezy. Loose, for a baggy sail -- downwind and/or calm.

14. *Spreaders* -- Crossbars on the mast to spread the angle the shrouds make with the mast and thereby increase their leverage.

15. *Telltales* -- The short pieces of yarn attached to the shrouds and the backstay. They show how the wind is striking the boat. The helmsman must constantly be checking the telltales on the *windward* side (the side of the boat that the wind is coming over). They indicate how the sails should be trimmed.

APPENDIX III

SAILING TERMS

1. *Windward* -- The direction *from* which the wind is blowing.

2. *Leeward* -- The direction *to* which the wind is blowing.

3. *Port and Starboard Tack* -- Opposite to the side the mainsail is on. If the mainsail is on the starboard side, the boat is on the port tack and vice-versa.

4. *To Tack* -- To change from the port tack to the starboard tack (or vice-versa) turning the bow of the boat into the wind. The command of preparation is "Ready About." The command of execution is "Hard Alee."

5. *To Jibe* -- To change from the port tack to the starboard tack (or vice-versa) turning the bow of the boat away from the wind (downwind). The command of preparation is "Prepare to Jibe" and the command of execution is "Jibe Ho." Imagine yourself on a boat. Face the wind. If you turn the boat so the bow swings through the direction you're facing, it's a tack. If you turn the boat the other way, it's a jibe. Remember the two "T's" -- *T*ack *T*owards (the wind).

6. *A Beat, To Beat, Beating* -- A series of tacks.

7. *Points of Sailing* -- Describing the direction of the boat in relation to the direction of the wind.
   a. *Closehauled* -- About 45 degrees from the wind.
   b. *Reach* -- About 90 degrees from the wind. Wind is "abeam."
   c. *Run* -- About 180 degrees from the wind. You are sailing "downwind."

8. *By the Lee* -- If the boat has been turned too far downwind, so that the wind is now coming over the same side of the boat that the main boom is on, you are sailing "by the lee." Risky.

9. *In Irons* -- When the boat is headed into the wind and has lost all forward motion it is "in irons." The rudder will no longer turn the boat (unless it is drifting backwards), since it works only by deflecting the passing water.

10. *True Wind* -- The actual direction the wind is blowing.

11. *Apparent Wind* -- The vector (change in wind direction) produced by the boat's forward speed.

12. *Weather Helm* -- The tendency of a boat to head into the wind if the helm is dropped.

13. *Lee Helm* -- The tendency of a boat to head away from the wind if the helm is dropped.

14. *A Header* -- A change in wind direction towards the bow of the boat.

15. *A Lift* -- A change in wind direction towards the stern of the boat. Remember that a header for a boat on the port tack is a lift for a boat on the starboard tack.

16. *Veering* -- A change in wind direction clockwise in relation to the compass. Northeast to East, for example.

17. *Backing* -- A change in wind direction counter-clockwise in relation to the compass. West to Southwest, for example.

18. *Bernouli's Principle* -- Simply that if the velocity of the air flowing past one side of an airfoil is greater than that on the other side, the pressure correspondingly decreases on the former side creating a suction like that which creates the lift of an airplane's wing and the pull of a boat's sail.

19. *Slot Effect* -- The funneling of air behind the mainsail through the slot formed between the main and the jib. This increases the velocity of the air on the lee side of the main, thereby increasing its suction and efficiency.

20. *Backwind* -- Caused by the slot being too narrow and forcing the funneled air into the backside of the main, rather than past it. Backwind makes the main appear to be luffing.

21. *Surfing* -- Being pushed by the motion of the wave, much like a surfboarder.

22. *Planing* -- Increased speed by skimming along the surface of the water. Depends upon the shape of the hull and the boat weight. Most keel boats cannot plane.

23. *Stability* -- The relation of the center of buoyancy to the center of gravity. The further apart they are, the greater the stability.

24. *Positive or Ultimate Stability* -- The boat with positive stability will always, like a cat, end right-side-up (unless she fills with water). Most cruising boats have positive stability, can be closed up tight so no water can enter, and have self-bailing cockpits.

25. *Hull Speed* -- The theoretical speed beyond which a displacement boat cannot go, usually $1.34\sqrt{LWL}$.

26. *Collision Course* -- If the relative bearing of the two converging yachts doesn't change, eventually they will collide.

APPENDIX IV

PROPER SAIL FOLDING

1. Fold foot over window.

2. With one hand anchoring cloth, reach upsail with the other.

3. Lifting and dragging the head toward you,

4. Fold it down over the window and foot.

5. Continue with these accordion-like folds,

6. Lifting and pulling the sail toward . . .

7. The growing pile of folds,

8. Until the head is reached.

12. All ready for tomorrow's sail.

11. Tack outside on jib, and you will be . . .

10. Starting so the clew will be outside on a mainsail,

9. Then roll up the pile in big folds,

APPENDIX V

ADDITIONAL KNOTS

Clove Hitch

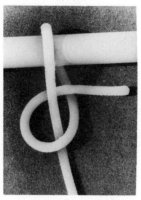

1. Around and over itself, around and under itself,

2. And you have a Clove Hitch

Two-Half Hitches

1. Around and through,

2. And around and through.

Rolling Hitch

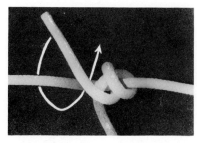

1. Try this one,

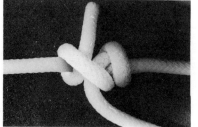

2. You'll like it . . .

Fast Bowline

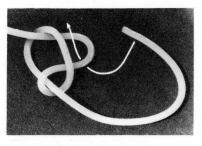

1. Feed free end through,

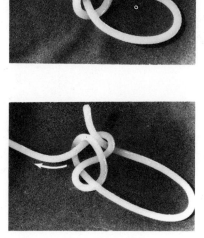

2. And pull the loop out . . .   3. Presto: a quick bowline.

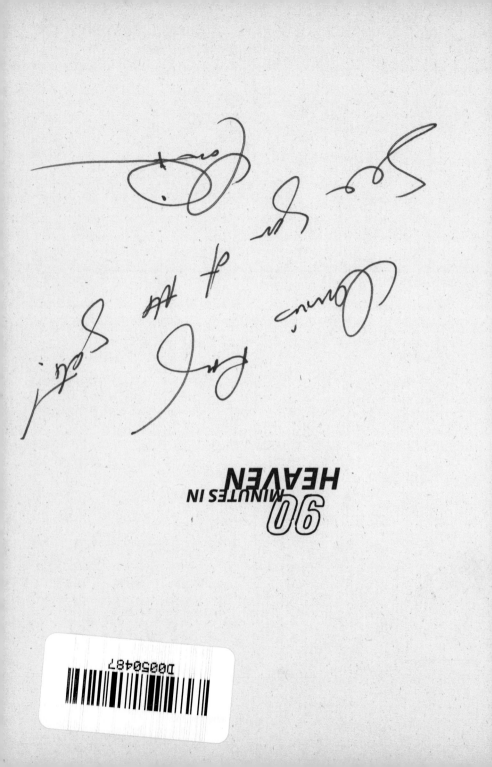

90
MINUTES IN
HEAVEN

A Special Edition for Young Readers

90 MINUTES IN HEAVEN

MY TRUE STORY

DON PIPER
WITH CECIL MURPHEY

Revell

a division of Baker Publishing Group
Grand Rapids, Michigan

Published by Revell
a division of Baker Publishing Group
P.O. Box 6287, Grand Rapids, MI 49516-6287
www.revellbooks.com

Printed in the United States of America

Library of Congress Cataloging-in-Publication Data
Piper, Don, 1950–
    90 minutes in heaven : my true story / Don Piper, with Cecil Murphey. —
 [Rev.], young readers ed.
        p. cm.
    ISBN 978-0-8007-3399-5 (pbk.)
    1. Heaven—Christianity—Juvenile literature. 2. Future life—Christianity—Juvenile literature. 3. Near-death experiences—Religious aspects—Christianity—Juvenile literature. 4. Death—Religious aspects—Christianity—Juvenile literature. I. Murphey, Cecil B. II. Title. III. Title: Ninety minutes in heaven.
    BT846.3.P56 2009
    231.7'3092—dc22   2009021455

Interior illustrations by Tim Foley.

12   13   14   15   16   9 8 7 6 5

To my children,
Nicole, Christopher, and Joseph—
all great gifts from God

CONTENTS

CONTENTS

PREFACE

I love kids. They are so full of life. They are all about possibilities. But they are also all about discovery.

Not long after we arrive here on earth, we find out that we don't get to stay. A classmate dies. A grandmother passes away. We might even lose a brother or sister, a mom or dad. That's what happened to sisters Riley and Tyler Knight. Riley and Tyler's parents were going to have two more children, but those children did not live. Their parents, Deidre and Jud Knight, are my agents who help me get my books published, including this one.

Not long ago my son, Chris, and I were to meet with the Knight family at a hotel in Jacksonville, Florida, to talk about new books I am writing. On the way to meet me, Deidre and Riley met a famous person in the eleva-

tor, comedian Chris Rock. Riley was so excited to meet such a famous person.

But Riley had some questions she wanted to ask me when she got off the elevator. Her mother had told her about my book *90 Minutes in Heaven: A True Story of Death & Life*. After meeting me, she said, "I've met *two* famous people today—Chris Rock and Don Piper!" Well, Chris Rock is famous. I'm not so sure about me. But something did happen to me that didn't happen to Chris Rock. I died and went to heaven, and then I was able to come back!

Because I went to heaven, Riley wanted to know what heaven is like. While we ate breakfast together, I told her about the many beautiful and amazing things I had seen, and that one day she would see the children in heaven that she had never met here on earth.

I receive many letters, phone calls, and emails from kids like you who want to know about heaven. Many of them have friends or family members who have died. These children want to know if they will see their loved ones again, and they want to know what they will see and do in heaven when they get there someday. I have tried to answer those questions in this special edition called *90 Minutes in Heaven: My True Story*.

But kids don't write or call me just to ask about heaven. Many young people want to know about how to help friends and loved ones who are sick. Some ask me about

problems at school. And some are very worried about their parents breaking up or making ends meet. One twelve-year-old recently wrote me to ask about "faith in dark times."

Often these letters are sad. Everyone, no matter what age they are, needs hope. This book will help you have hope—hope for eternal life, and hope for a better life now!

God has blessed me with wonderful parents, a beautiful wife, three very fine children, and a new granddaughter named Carlee. I also have brothers and many friends. I love these people here on earth, but I want to be with them all in heaven someday. And though you and I have not even met, I would like to see you there too.

As you will discover from reading this book, I went to heaven when I died because I knew the way to heaven. Jesus is the way! I came to accept Jesus as my Savior when I was not much older than you are. And I found that in heaven there is no pain or loneliness or sadness or tears or darkness or failure. Heaven is a perfect place. You will love it there. (Riley Knight, I will see you there, and we'll meet our other brothers and sisters who loved the Lord too.)

Yes, heaven is real, and Jesus is the way.

Don Piper
March 2009

ACKNOWLEDGMENTS

I want to thank Lonnie Hull DuPont for helping me make this book kid-friendly. And I want to thank Baker Publishing Group, Revell, and Dr. Vicki Crumpton for caring about kids so much that they would publish a book like this one. I also thank you for reading this book. May God give you a long and happy life.

PROLOGUE

I died on January 18, 1989.

Paramedics reached the scene of the accident within minutes. They found no pulse and declared me dead. They covered me with a tarp so that onlookers wouldn't stare at me while they attended to the injuries of the others. I was completely unaware of the paramedics or anyone else around me.

Immediately after I died, I went straight to heaven.

While I was in heaven, a preacher came on the accident scene. Even though he knew I was dead, he rushed to my lifeless body and prayed for me. Despite the scoffing of the emergency medical technicians (EMTs), he refused to stop praying.

At least ninety minutes after the EMTs pronounced me dead, God answered that man's prayers.

I returned to earth.

This is my story.

1
THE ACCIDENT

The Baptist General Convention of Texas holds annual statewide conferences. In January 1989, I attended.

The conference started on Monday and was scheduled to end on Wednesday. On Tuesday night, I joined a friend named J. V. Thomas for a long walk. We walked and talked for about an hour despite the cold, rainy weather. J. V. remembers that time well.

So do I, but for a different reason: it would be the last time I would ever walk normally.

✝

On Wednesday morning the weather got worse. A steady rain fell.

I had packed the night before, so everything was stowed in my red Ford Escort. As soon as we finished, I said good-bye to all my friends and got into my car to drive back to the church where I was on staff, South Park Baptist Church in Alvin, near Houston.

When I started the engine, I remembered that three weeks earlier I had received a traffic ticket for not wearing a seat belt. A Texas trooper had caught me. Until I received the ticket, I had not usually worn a seat belt, but after that I changed my ways.

So I fastened my seat belt. That small act would be a crucial decision.

There were two ways to get back to Houston and on to Alvin. Each choice is probably about the same distance. That morning I decided to take the Gulf Freeway.

Many times since then I've thought about my decision to take the Gulf Freeway. It's amazing how we pay no attention to simple decisions at the time they're made. Yet even the smallest decisions often hold significant consequences. This was one of those choices.

I didn't have to drive far before I reached Lake Livingston, a large, beautiful lake. Spanning it is a two-lane highway built up above the level of the lake and extremely narrow. I would have to drive across a long expanse of water on that narrow road until I reached the other side.

At the end of the highway across the lake is a bridge. Immediately after the bridge, the road rises sharply. It

was a dangerous bridge, and as I would learn later, several accidents had occurred on it.

The steady rain had turned into a downpour. At 11:45 a.m., just before I cleared the east end of the bridge, an eighteen-wheeler semitruck weaved across the center line and hit my car head-on. The truck sandwiched my small car between the bridge railing and the driver's side of the truck.

All those wheels went right on top of my car and smashed it.

I remember parts of the accident, but most of my information came from the accident report and people at the scene. From the description I've received from witnesses, the truck then veered off to the other side of the narrow bridge and sideswiped two other cars. Although shaken up, both drivers suffered only minor cuts and bruises.

Because of the truck's speed, the accident report states that the impact was about 110 miles an hour. That is, the truck struck me while going sixty miles an hour, and I was going fifty.

After the accident, the truck driver didn't have a scratch on him. The truck received little damage. However, the heavy vehicle had crushed my Ford and pushed it from the narrow road. Only the bridge railing stopped my car from going into the lake.

Medical backup arrived a few minutes later. Someone examined me, found no pulse, and declared that I had been killed instantly.

I have no recollection of the impact or anything that happened afterward.

In one powerful, overwhelming second, I died.

2
MY TIME IN HEAVEN

When I died, I had no sense of fading away or of coming back. I never felt my body being transported. I heard no voices calling to me or anything else. At the same time as my last recollection of seeing the bridge and the rain, a light enveloped me with a brilliance beyond description. Only that.

In my next moment of awareness, I was standing in heaven.

Joy filled me as I looked around. I became aware of a large crowd of people in front of a brilliant, ornate gate.

The crowd rushed toward me. I didn't see Jesus, but I did see people I had known. As they surged toward me, I

knew that all of them had died during my lifetime. Their presence seemed absolutely natural.

Every person was smiling, shouting, and praising God. Although no one said so, I knew they were my welcoming committee. It was as if they had all gathered just outside heaven's gate, waiting for me.

The first person I recognized was my grandfather. He looked exactly as I remembered him, with his shock of white hair and what I called a big banana nose. He stopped and stood in front of me. A grin covered his face.

"Donnie!" (That's what my grandfather always called me.) His eyes lit up, and he held out his arms and embraced me, holding me tightly. He was once again the robust, strong grandfather I had remembered as a child.

After being hugged by my grandfather, I don't remember who was second or third. The crowd surrounded me. Some hugged me and a few kissed my cheek, while others pumped my hand. Never had I felt more loved.

One person in that greeting committee was Mike Wood, my childhood friend. Mike was special because he had invited me to Sunday school and was influential in my becoming a Christian.

Mike was the most devoted young Christian I knew. He was also a popular kid and had lettered four years in football, basketball, and track and field. He became a hero to me, because he lived the Christian lifestyle he often talked about.

When he was nineteen, Mike was killed in a car wreck. It broke my heart when I heard about his death, and it took me a long time to get over it. His death was the biggest shock and most painful experience I'd had up to that time in my life.

Now I saw Mike in heaven. As he slipped his arm around my shoulder, my grief vanished. Never had I seen Mike smile so brightly.

More and more people reached for me and called me by name. I felt overwhelmed by the number of people who had come to welcome me to heaven. There were so many of them, and I had never imagined anyone being as happy as they were. All were full of life and joy.

I saw my great-grandfather, heard his voice, and felt his embrace as he told me how excited he was that I had come to join them.

I saw Barry Wilson, who had been my classmate in high school but later drowned in a lake. Barry hugged me, and his smile radiated a happiness I didn't know was possible. He and everyone who followed praised God and told me how excited they were to see me and to welcome me to heaven.

I spotted two teachers who had loved me and often talked to me about Christ.

As I walked among all these people, I became aware of the wide variety of ages—old and young and every age in between. Many of them hadn't known each other on

earth, but each had influenced my life in some way. Even though they hadn't met on earth, they seemed to know each other now.

Everyone continually embraced me, touched me, spoke to me, laughed, and praised God. This seemed to go on for a long time, but I didn't tire of it.

My father is one of eleven children. Some of his brothers and sisters had as many as thirteen children. When I was a kid, our family reunions were so huge we rented an entire city park. We Pipers are affectionate, with a lot of hugging and kissing whenever we come together. None of those earthly family reunions, however, prepared me for the gathering I experienced at the gates of heaven.

Heaven was many things, but without a doubt, it was the greatest family reunion of all.

I had never felt such powerful embraces or feasted my eyes on such beauty. Heaven's warm, radiant light engulfed me. I could hardly grasp the vivid, dazzling colors. I felt as if I had never seen, heard, or felt anything so real before. Never, even in my happiest moments, had I ever felt so fully alive.

I stood speechless in front of the crowd of loved ones, trying to take in everything. Over and over I heard how excited they were to have me among them. I knew they had been waiting and expecting me, yet I also knew that in heaven there is no sense of time passing.

I gazed at the faces again as I realized that they all had contributed to my becoming a Christian or had encour-

aged me in my growth as a believer. Each one had affected me. I knew that because of their influence, I was able to be present with them in heaven.

Still overwhelmed, I didn't know how to respond to their welcoming words. "I'm happy to be with you," I said, and even those words couldn't express the joy of being surrounded and embraced by all those people I loved.

I wasn't conscious of anything I'd left behind and felt no regrets about leaving family or possessions. It was as if God had removed any worries from my mind, and I could only rejoice at being together with these wonderful people. They looked exactly as I once knew them—although they were more radiant and joyful than they'd ever been on earth.

My great-grandmother was Native American. As a child I saw her only after she had developed osteoporosis. Her head and shoulders were bent forward, giving her a humped appearance. I especially remember her extremely wrinkled face. The other thing that stands out in my memory is that she had false teeth—which she didn't wear often.

Yet when she smiled at me in heaven, her teeth sparkled. I knew they were her own, and when she smiled, it was the most beautiful smile I had ever seen. Then I noticed something else—she wasn't slumped over. She stood strong and upright, and the wrinkles had been erased from her face.

As I stared at her beaming face, I sensed that age has no meaning in heaven. All of the people I encountered

were the same age they had been the last time I had seen them—except that in heaven every feature was perfect, beautiful, and wonderful to gaze at.

No matter which direction I looked, I saw someone I had loved and who had loved me. They surrounded me, moving around so that everyone had a chance to welcome me to heaven.

I felt more loved than ever before in my life.

At some point, I looked around, and coming from the gate—a short distance ahead—was a brilliance that was brighter than the light that surrounded us. As soon as I stopped gazing at faces, I realized that everything around me glowed with intense brightness.

We began to move toward that light. No one said it was time to do so, and yet we all started forward at the same time.

As I stared ahead, everything seemed to grow taller— like a gentle hill that kept going upward and never stopped. As far ahead as I could see, there was absolutely nothing but intense, radiant light.

I didn't know how it could get more dazzling, but it did. The farther I walked, the brighter the light. I had the sense that I was being ushered into the presence of God.

A holy awe came over me as I stepped forward. I had no idea what lay ahead, but I sensed that with each step I took, it would grow more wondrous.

Then I heard the music.

3 HEAVENLY MUSIC

Although I was aware of the joyous sounds and melodies that filled the air, I never saw anything that produced the sound. I had the sense that whatever made the heavenly music was just above me, but I didn't look up. I asked no questions and never wondered about anything. Everything was perfect. I had no questions to ask.

Sounds filled my mind and heart. It's difficult to explain them. The most amazing one, however, was the angels' wings.

I didn't see them, but the sound was a beautiful melody that seemed never to stop. The whooshing of wings resounded as if it was a form of never-ending praise. As I listened, I simply *knew* what it was.

A second sound remains, even today—the single, most vivid memory I have of my entire heavenly experience. I call it music, but it differed from anything I had ever heard on earth.

Hundreds of songs were being sung at the same time. I heard them from every direction and realized that each voice praised God.

I write *voice*, but it was more than that. Some sounded instrumental, but I wasn't sure—and I wasn't concerned. All of it was musical—melodies and tones I'd never experienced before. "Hallelujah!" "Praise!" "Glory to God!" "Praise to the King!" Such words rang out in all the music.

If we played three CDs of praise at the same time, we'd have noise that would drive us crazy. This was totally different. Every sound blended, and each voice or instrument enhanced the others. I could clearly distinguish each song. It sounded as if each praise hymn was meant for me to hear.

Later I realized that none of the hymns were about Jesus' sacrifice or death. All were praises about Christ's reign as King of Kings and how wonderful he is.

I marveled at the glorious music. Even now, back on earth, sometimes I still hear faint echoes of that music. When I'm especially tired and lie in bed with my eyes closed, occasionally I drift off to sleep with the sounds of heaven filling my mind.

I cherish those sounds, and at times I think, *I can't wait to hear them again—in person*. It's what I look forward to. I want to see everybody again, but I know I'll be with them forever. Most of all, I want to hear those songs again.

In those minutes—and they held no sense of time for me—others touched me, and their warm embraces were absolutely real. I saw colors I would never have believed existed. I've never felt more alive than I did then.

I was home. I was where I belonged. I wanted to be there more than I had ever wanted to be anywhere on earth. Time had slipped away, and I was simply present in heaven. All worries, anxieties, and concerns vanished. I had no needs, and I felt perfect.

After a time (I'm resorting to human terms again), we started moving together right up to the gate. No one said it, but I simply knew God had sent all those people to escort me inside the portals of heaven.

Looming just over the heads of my reception committee stood an awesome gate interrupting a wall that faded out of sight in both directions. The actual entrance was small in comparison to the massive gate itself. I stared, but I couldn't see the ends of the wall in either direction. I couldn't see the top either.

The Bible refers to the gates of pearl. The gate wasn't made of pearls, but to me, it looked as if someone had spread pearl icing on a cake. The gate glowed and shimmered.

I paused just outside the gate, and I could see inside. It was like a city with streets paved with gold bricks. That's as close as I can come to describing what lay inside the gate. Everything I saw was bright—the brightest colors my eyes had ever seen.

I continued to step closer to the gate and assumed that I would go inside. My friends and relatives were all in front of me, calling, urging, and inviting me to follow.

The music increased. The closer we got, the more intense, alive, and vivid everything became.

As I reached the gate, I paused—I'm not sure why. I wanted to go inside. I knew everything would be even more thrilling than what I had experienced so far.

Then, just as suddenly as I had arrived at the gates of heaven, I left them.

4
FROM HEAVEN TO EARTH

The EMTs pronounced me dead as soon as they arrived at the scene. They stated that I died instantly.

According to the report, the collision occurred at 11:45 a.m. The EMTs became so busy working with the others involved that it was about 1:15 p.m. before they were ready to move me. They checked for a pulse once again.

I was still dead.

The state law said they had to pronounce me dead officially before they could remove my body from the scene of the accident. They had called for the Jaws of Life to get me out of the smashed car. (The Jaws of Life is a brand of

piston-rod hydraulic tools that are used to pry trapped victims from crashed vehicles.)

Because I was dead, there seemed to be no need for speed. Their concern focused on clearing the bridge for traffic to flow again.

When the truck came in at an angle and went right over the top of me, the truck smashed the car's ceiling, and the dashboard came down across my legs, crushing my right leg. My left leg was shattered in two places between the car seat and the dashboard. My left arm went over the top of my head, was dislocated, and swung backward over the seat. It was still attached—barely.

That arm had been lying on the driver's side door, because I had been driving with my right hand. As I would learn later, the major bones were now missing, so my lower left arm was just a piece of flesh that held my hand to the rest of my arm.

It was the same with the left leg. There was some tissue just above my knee that still fed blood to the calf and foot below. Four and a half inches of femur (the thighbone) were missing and never found. The doctors have no medical explanation why I didn't lose all the blood in my body.

Glass and blood had sprayed everywhere. I had all kinds of small holes in my face from embedded glass. The steering wheel had pounded into my chest. Blood seeped out of my eyes, ears, and nose.

The EMTs covered me with a waterproof tarp that also blocked off the top of the car. They made no attempt to move me or try to get me out immediately—they couldn't have anyway, because it would have been impossible for them to drag or lift me out of the vehicle without the Jaws of Life.

Police halted all traffic on the bridge and waited for the ambulance to arrive. While they waited, traffic backed up for miles in both directions.

Dick and Anita Onerecker came upon the scene of the accident. Dick and Anita had both spoken at the conference I'd just attended. For years I had heard of Dick Onerecker, but that conference was the first time I had ever seen him.

Before the Onereckers reached the bridge, the accident had occurred and traffic had started to back up. People got out of their cars and milled around, asking questions. After Dick and Anita got out of their car, they asked fellow drivers, "What's going on up there?"

The word had passed down that there had been a serious auto accident. "A truck crashed into a car" was about all anyone knew.

Dick and Anita stood around a few minutes. Sometime between 12:30 and 12:45 p.m., they decided to walk to the accident site. When they saw a police officer, Dick said, "I'm a minister. Is there anyone here I can help? Is there anyone I can pray for?"

The police officer shook his head. "The man in the red car is deceased."

Dick would later tell it this way: "God spoke to me and said, 'You need to pray for the man in the red car.'"

I can't do that, Dick thought. *The man is dead.*

Dick stared at the officer, knowing that what he would say wouldn't make sense. Yet God spoke to him so clearly that he had no doubt about what he was to do. God had told him to pray for a dead man.

"I'd like to pray for the man in the red car," Dick finally said to the officer.

"Like I said, he's dead."

"I know this sounds strange, but I want to pray for him anyway."

The officer stared at him a long time before he finally said, "Well, you know, if that's what you want to do, go ahead, but I've got to tell you it's an awful sight. He's dead, and it's really a mess under the tarp. Blood and glass are everywhere, and the body's all mangled."

"Thanks," Dick said, and walked to the tarp-covered car.

From the pictures of that smashed-down car, it's almost impossible to believe, but somehow Dick actually crawled into the trunk of my Ford. It was a hatchback, but that part of the car had been severed. I was still covered by the tarp, which he didn't remove, so it was extremely dark inside the car.

34

Dick crept in behind me, leaned over the backseat, and put his hand on my right shoulder. He began praying for me. As he said later, "I felt compelled to pray. I didn't know who the man was or whether he was a believer. I knew only that God told me I had to pray for him."

As Dick prayed, he became quite emotional and broke down and cried several times. Then he sang. Dick had an excellent voice and often sang publicly. He paused several times to sing a hymn and then went back to prayer.

Not only did Dick believe God had called him to pray for me, but he prayed quite specifically that I would be delivered from unseen injuries, meaning brain and internal injuries.

This sounds strange, because Dick knew I was dead. Not only had the police officer told him, but he also had checked for a pulse. He had no idea why he prayed as he did, except God told him to. He didn't pray for the injuries he could see, only for the healing of internal damage. He said he prayed the most passionate, fervent, emotional prayer of his life. As I would later learn, Dick was a highly emotional man anyway.

Then he began to sing again. "O what peace we often forfeit, O what needless pain we bear, all because we do not carry everything to God in prayer!" The only thing I personally know for certain about the entire event is that as he sang the old hymn "What a Friend We Have in Jesus," I began to sing with him.

In that moment, I was aware of two things. First, I was singing—a different kind of singing than the tones of heaven. I heard my own voice and then became aware of someone else singing.

The second thing I was aware of was that someone clutched my hand. It was a strong, powerful touch and the first physical sensation I experienced with my return to earthly life.

More than a year would pass before I understood the significance of that hand clasping mine.

5
EARTH TO HOSPITAL

I'm not certain what the world record is for exiting a wrecked car, but Dick Onerecker must have surely broken it that Wednesday afternoon. When a dead man began to sing with him, Dick scrambled out of that smashed car and raced over to the nearest EMT.

"The man's alive! He's not dead! He's alive!"

The EMT stared.

Dick could only keep yelling, "He's singing! He's alive!"

"Oh really?" the paramedic asked. "We know a dead guy when we see him. That guy is *dead*."

"I'm telling you, that man just sang with me. He's alive."

The man turned away from Dick and refused to go over to my car.

Dick walked over to the remaining ambulance and said to the driver, "That man is alive. Go look at him."

"He's dead."

"Then humor me. Just feel his pulse," Dick pleaded.

"Okay, we'll check on him for you," the man said. He walked over to the car, raised the tarp, reached inside, and found my right arm. He felt my pulse.

Everyone leaped into action. They began trying to figure out how to get me out. They could have taken me out on one side, but it would have been without my left leg. I'm not sure they could have gotten my right leg out either.

The point is that even though they could have gotten me out without the equipment, they would have left some of me in the car. They decided to wait on the proper equipment. They got on the phone and ordered the Jaws of Life to hurry from Huntsville, which was at least thirty miles away.

I'm sure they did whatever they could for me, but I remember nothing. I heard voices, but I couldn't make sense of anything they said. Dick refused to leave me. He continued to pray until the Jaws of Life arrived. Only after they lifted me into the ambulance did he leave my side.

When the EMTs lifted me out of the car, I remember one of them said something about being careful so that my left leg didn't come off.

My system was in shock, so I felt no pain—not then, anyway. That came later.

I remember thinking, *Something terrible has happened here, and I think it's happened to me.* Even when I knew they were moving me into the ambulance, I felt weightless.

I vaguely remember when they pulled up at the Huntsville Hospital, a fairly large regional medical center. It was about 2:30 p.m.

I was aware of being wheeled into the hospital. They took me into a room where a doctor was waiting for me. He spent quite a while checking me over. "Mr. Piper, we're going to do everything we can to save you," he must have said three times. "You're hurt bad, seriously hurt, but we'll do all we can."

I later learned that he didn't expect me to survive. But he did everything he could to give me hope and urge me to fight to stay alive. Several people moved around me. They were obviously trying to save my life, but I still felt no pain.

"We have your wife on the phone," someone said. A nurse laid the phone beside my ear, and I remember talking to Eva, but I can't recall one word either of us said.

My condition was deteriorating rapidly, and they didn't know if I was going to survive the afternoon. The medical team put me back inside an ambulance for the eighty-mile trip to Houston. Hermann Hospital was the only place for me if I was to have any chance to survive.

"How fast do I go?" the driver asked the attendant who sat next to me in the ambulance.

"Put the pedal to the metal! We've got to get there—*now*!"

Before we started the trip, I still had felt no pain. I was in and out of consciousness. I felt weightless, as if my mind had no connection with my body. However, about ten minutes down the road, a slight throbbing began.

At first, I became aware of a tiny pain in my left arm. Then my left leg throbbed. My head started to ache. Within minutes I hurt in so many places, it felt as if every part of my body had been wounded, punched, or beaten. Each beat of my heart felt like sledgehammers pounding every inch of my body.

The vehicle rocked back and forth, in and out of traffic, and the siren blared. It was the most painful, nightmarish trip of my life. I passed out several times from the pain.

We finally arrived at the emergency room in Houston at Hermann Hospital at 6:20 p.m. Six and a half hours had passed from the time of the accident.

By the time I reached the hospital in Houston, thousands of people were praying. Members in hundreds of churches prayed for my recovery. For the next few days, word spread about my injuries, and more people prayed. Over the years, I've met many of those who asked God to spare my life. The prayers were effective: I lived, and I'm still alive.

As the EMTs lifted my gurney out of the ambulance, I spotted Eva's face. I stared into her eyes. I sensed that she feared I wouldn't live.

That's when I knew I must have been in really bad shape—and I was. My chest had already turned purple, and medics had bandaged almost every part of my body. Tiny pieces of glass were embedded in my face, chest, and head. I was aware that tiny shards had fallen out of my skin and rested on the gurney next to my head.

No one had to tell me that I looked hideous. Anyone who knew me wouldn't have recognized me. I wondered how Eva had known who I was.

My pain was off the scale. Once inside the trauma center, a nurse gave me a shot of morphine—and then followed up with several more shots. Nothing helped. Nothing dulled the pain.

Shortly after my arrival at Hermann, they sent me to surgery, where I remained for eleven hours. Under anesthesia, I finally felt no pain.

By the time I was conscious again, it was Thursday morning. When I opened my eyes, one nurse was cleaning my wounds while another was putting me into traction. I could feel that she was putting rods between my ankle and my arm. I heard myself scream. I hurt more than I thought was humanly possible.

I just wanted relief.

✝

When Dick Onerecker came to see me two weeks after the accident, I had just been moved from the intensive care unit (ICU) to a hospital room. He told me about God telling him to pray for me and that he had done that for several minutes.

"The best news is that I don't have any brain damage or any internal injuries," I said.

Dick chuckled. "Of course you don't. That's what God told me to pray for, and God answered."

"You believed that? You believed that God would answer that prayer?"

"Yes, I did," he said. "I knew with all the other injuries you had that God was going to answer my prayer."

It took a few seconds for me to absorb what he'd said. "I'll tell you this," I said. "I know I had internal injuries, but somewhere between that bridge and this hospital I don't anymore."

Tears ran down Dick's face, and he said, "I know. I wish I could pray like that all the time."

6
THE RECOVERY BEGINS

Pain became my constant companion. For a long time I would not know what it was like not to hurt all over my body.

Despite that, within a few days of the accident, I began to realize how many miracles had occurred. I refer to them as miracles because I believe there are no accidents or surprises with God.

First, I wore my seat belt.

Second, the accident happened on the bridge. What if it had happened on the open highway across the lake when I was headed toward the bridge? My car would have plunged down into the lake, and I would have drowned.

Third, I had no head injuries. Anyone who saw me or read the medical report said it was impossible that I suffered no brain damage. (Eva still jokes that on occasion she's not so sure I didn't.) Just as bewildering to all the medical people was that the accident affected none of my internal organs. That fact defied all medical explanation.

Fourth, orthopedic surgeon Dr. Tom Greider, who was on duty at Hermann Hospital that day, saved my leg. Dr. Greider "just happened to be" one of the few experts in the United States who deals with such bizarre trauma. He chose to use a fairly new, experimental procedure, the Ilizarov frame. He performed the surgery one week after my accident.

The implanted Ilizarov not only saved my leg, but it also allowed the doctors to lengthen the bone in my left leg after I had lost four and a half inches of my femur in the accident. The femur is the largest bone in the human body and quite difficult to break.

When Dr. Greider examined me, he faced a choice. He could use the Ilizarov frame or amputate my leg. Even if he chose to use the Ilizarov frame, there was no guarantee that I would not lose the leg. In fact, at that stage, he wasn't even certain I would pull through the ordeal. A less-skilled and less-committed doctor might have amputated, assuming it wouldn't make much difference because I would die anyway.

Fifth, people prayed for me. I have thousands of cards, letters, and prayer-grams—many from people I don't know in places I've never been who prayed for me because they heard of the accident. I've since had people tell me that this experience changed their belief in the power of prayer.

On the night I entered Hermann Trauma Center, I was in surgery for eleven hours. I had the broken bone in my right leg set. My left forearm had to be stabilized because two inches of each bone were missing. My left leg was put into traction because four and a half inches of femur were missing.

I lay on my bed with needles everywhere, unable to move, dependent on the life-support equipment. I could barely see over the top of my oxygen mask. During those days in the ICU, sometimes I'd wake up and wonder, *Am I really here, or am I just imagining this?*

I had experienced heaven, returned to earth, and then suffered through more pain than I ever thought possible. It would be a long time before my condition or my attitude changed. Living in the ICU was horrible. They were doing the best they could, but the pain never let up.

"God, is this what I came back for?" I cried out many times. "You brought me back to earth for this?"

I had to lie flat on my back because of the missing bone in my left leg. (They never found the bone. Apparently, it was ejected from the car into the lake when my leg was

crushed between the car seat and dashboard.) Because of having to lie flat, my lungs filled with fluid.

On my sixth day, I was so near death that the hospital called my family to come to see me. I had developed double pneumonia, and they didn't think I would make it through the night.

I had survived the injuries. Now I was dying of pneumonia.

That's when the miracle of prayer really began to work. Hundreds of people had been praying for me since they learned of the accident, and I knew that. Yet, at that point, nothing had seemed to make any difference.

Eva called my best friend, David Gentiles. "Please come and see Don. He needs you," she said.

Without any hesitation, my friend drove nearly two hundred miles to see me. The nursing staff allowed him into my room in ICU for only five minutes.

Those minutes changed my life.

As I lay there with little hope of recovery—no one had suggested I'd ever be normal again—I didn't want to live. Not only did I face the ordeal of never-lessening pain, but I had been to heaven and wanted to return to that glorious place. *Take me back, God*, I prayed. *Please take me back.*

God's answer to that prayer was no.

When David entered my room, he clasped my fingers because they were all he could hold.

46

"You're going to make it," David said. "You have to make it. You've made it this far."

"I'm not sure. I . . . I don't know if I want to make it."

"You have to. If not for yourself, then hold on for us."

"I'm out of gas," I said. "I've done all I can. I've given it all I can. I don't have anything else to give."

"You have to make it. We won't let you go."

"I'm tired. I've fought all I can and I'm ready to die."

"We won't let you die. You understand that, Don? We won't let you give up."

"Just let me go—"

"No. You're going to live. Do you hear that? We won't let you die."

"If I live," I finally said, "it'll be because you want me to."

"We're going to pray," he said. "We're going to pray all night. I'm going to call everybody I know who can pray. I want you to know that those of us who care for you are going to stay up all night in prayer for you."

"Okay."

"We're going to do this for you, Don. You don't have to do anything. We're taking over from here. All you have to do is just lie there and let it happen. We're going to pray you through this."

David kissed me on the forehead and left.

An all-night prayer vigil followed. That vigil marked a turning point in my treatment and another series of miracles.

The pneumonia was gone the next day. They had prayed it away.

On that seventh day, in another long surgery, Dr. Greider installed the Ilizarov device so that I could sit up and receive breathing treatments.

When I awakened after another twelve hours of surgery, on my left leg was a massive stainless steel halo from my hip to just below my knee.

I became aware of Eva sitting next to my bed. "What is that?" I asked.

"We need to talk about it," she said. "It's a bone-growth device. We call it a fixator. It's the only chance for the doctors to save your left leg," she said.

I spotted wires leading from the device. "Are those wires going through my leg?"

"Yes. It's a new technique. They're trying to save your leg."

I didn't know enough to comment. I nodded and tried to relax.

Little did I know that nearly a year later I would still be staring at that device.

7
DECISIONS AND CHALLENGES

The Ilizarov frame may have sounded like a common procedure. It was far from that.

Initially this device was used to stretch legs. It forces the bone in the leg to grow while keeping the surrounding tissue intact.

The Ilizarov bone-growth device is what's called an external fixator. A Siberian doctor named Ilizarov invented it. Dr. Ilizarov experimented on sheep to develop a way to grow missing bones or lengthen short bones.

Missing-bone cases like mine involve breaking a limb with a clean break. Wires about the size of piano wire

are placed through the skin and bone, and they exit out the other side.

Six rods also went through the top of my left arm and came out the other side. Big stainless steel bars were placed above and below the arm to stabilize it, because both forearm bones were missing. The rods were the size of a pencil.

The femur Ilizarov device was anchored to my hip by rods that were also about the size of a pencil. The doctors drilled holes for four large rods from my groin to the side of my left hip. After they did that, I had at least thirty holes in my left leg. Many of them went completely through my leg and out the other side. The larger ones just went into the flesh, and rods were embedded in the pelvis.

Every day someone would come in and turn the screws on the Ilizarov device to stretch the bones. The Ilizarov device worked—and it was also the most painful process I endured as part of my recovery.

The stainless steel Ilizarov on my leg weighed about thirty pounds, and the external fixator on my arm probably weighed another twenty. Whether I was in my wheelchair (about eight months), on my rolling walker (three more months), or eventually my crutches (four more months), I carried that extra weight around for nearly a year.

Can you imagine the strange stares I received everywhere I went? People gasped and gawked at a man in a wheelchair with steel rods sticking out all over his body.

I've often kidded others that because of all this "metal-work," if archaeologists discover my body years from now, they'll think they've found a new species! My anatomy has been completely rearranged.

My right knee had been crushed, and I wore a cast on it for quite some time. They put a small, mesh basket around the kneecap so it would heal. My right arm was the only limb that didn't break.

Never again will I take simple physical ability for granted. During my recovery, even the tiniest movement was a miracle. Every time I relearned how to do something, it felt like an achievement.

Even with the success of the Ilizarov frame, however, the pain didn't leave—not for one minute.

I wanted to know how long I'd have to endure the device, how long before I'd know if it worked, how long before I'd walk again. No one would—or could—give me an answer, but I kept asking anyway.

"A few months" was the usual answer.

"How few?" I persisted.

One of the doctors finally said, "Many months. Maybe longer."

"You mean a few years?"

"Yes, perhaps years."

"And there's no guarantee that I'm going to be able to keep these limbs?"

"There's no guarantee. An infection could come on suddenly, and we'd be forced to remove your leg."

"You mean I could endure this for months and still end up with no leg?"

He nodded.

Obviously, that wasn't what I wanted to hear.

I kept seeking a guarantee that I would fully recover. I wanted assurance that I would be well. I wanted to be normal again. I wanted to be able to walk out of the hospital on my own two legs and go back to my former way of life. No one was willing—or able—to give me those assurances.

During the months after I received the Ilizarov frame, I had other problems. I developed infections—several times. Each time, I faced the reality that it might rage through my body and I would wake up without my leg.

Many nights I prayed, *God, take me back to heaven. I don't know why you brought me back to earth. Please don't leave me here.*

God's answer to that prayer was still no.

In the months and years ahead, I slowly understood at least some of the reasons I had returned to earth.

The healing process had begun. As I lay in that hospital bed day after day, I kept thinking of the words of David Gentiles. He and others had cried out in prayer for me to live.

I was in Hermann ICU for twelve days. Then I stayed four or five days in Hermann Hospital before they transferred me down the street to St. Luke's Hospital, where I remained for 105 days. Once I was home, I lay in bed for thirteen months and had thirty-four surgeries. I am still alive because numerous people, many of whom I've never met, prayed for me.

That's perhaps the biggest miracle: *people prayed, and God honored their prayers.*

I knew I wasn't going to die.

God's people wouldn't let me.

8
PAIN AND ADJUSTMENTS

Even though they didn't realize it, visitors made my situation worse. They cared for me and wanted to express that concern. Because they cared, they did the most natural thing in the world—they visited my hospital room. That was the problem.

The constant flow in and out of my room exhausted me. I felt I couldn't simply lie there and allow them to sit with me or talk to me. So on many days, I smiled and chatted with them when all I really wanted to do was collapse. Sometimes the pain made it almost impossible for me to be a good host, but I still tried. I kept reminding myself that they cared and had made an effort to see me, and I

didn't want to hurt anyone's feelings by asking them to leave or not to come.

Besides the pain and the flow of people in and out of my room, no matter how hard I tried, I couldn't enjoy living again. I wanted to go back to heaven. I prayed and others prayed with me, but a sense of despair began to set in. "Is it worth all this?" I asked several times every day.

How could I put into words that I had had the most joyful, powerful experience of my life? As close as Eva and I are, I couldn't tell even her at that time.

Going to heaven had been too sacred, too special.

The longer I lay in bed, the more convinced I became that I had nothing to look forward to. Heaven had been perfect—so beautiful and joyful.

When people came to see me, their words and gazes made me feel as if they were saying, "You're the most pitiful thing I've ever seen."

I guess I was.

I was the father of three children, the husband of a wonderful wife, and, until the accident, a man with a great future. I was thirty-eight years old when the accident happened and, up to that point, in great physical shape.

Within days after my accident, I knew I would never be that healthy man again. Now I was utterly helpless. I couldn't do anything for myself, not even lift my hand. Deep inside, I feared I would be helpless for the rest of my life. Friends, family, and medical personnel found ways of

providing for all of my physical needs, but I could only think of myself as being completely, utterly helpless.

I've tried to explain it this way: "Imagine yourself lying in bed. You have rods through your arms and wires through your legs, and you're on your back. You can't turn over. In fact, just to move your shoulder a quarter of an inch is impossible unless you reach up and grab what looks like a trapeze bar that hangs above your bed. You are completely immobile."

I began to break out with bedsores on my back due to being in one position too long. So the hospital provided a special waterbed that constantly moved. The only time I ever left the room was when they wheeled me down to X-ray.

The worst daily torment took place when a nurse cleaned the pinholes where the wires went into my skin. All the nurses who treated me had to be taught how to clean those pinholes. Because they didn't want the skin to stick to the wire, they had to keep breaking the skin when it attached itself—as it did occasionally. Then the nurse forced hydrogen peroxide down each pinhole to prevent infection.

I could think of nothing worse to endure, and it happened every day.

And that wasn't all. Four times a day, every six hours, they'd take a wrench and turn screws on the device. It didn't matter whether it was day or night, every six hours

someone came into my room to turn the screws. The idea was that this would stretch the ends of the bones inside the leg and eventually cause the growing bone to replace the missing bone. The turn hurt beyond description.

Perhaps the worst part for me was that I never slept. For eleven and a half months I never went to sleep—I just passed out. Even with morphine, I was never pain free. If I made the slightest effort to move, a wire embedded in my flesh would tear my skin.

After a while, I learned to live with that situation, but I never got used to it.

✝

Eventually I was able to do something doctors said I would never be able to do: I learned to walk again.

They had warned me that because of the broken knee in my right leg, and the loss of the femur in my left (even with a replaced-and-stretched bone in place), I would not walk again, and if I did, I would be wearing heavy braces.

At some point, they put me in what I referred to as a Frankenstein bed. They strapped me to a large board and turned the bed so that my feet were on the floor and I was in a standing position, although still strapped to the bed. Two physical therapists placed a large belt around my waist and walked on either side of me.

My legs had grown extremely weak, so they helped me take my first steps. It took me days to learn to stand

again so that I could put weight on my own legs. I had grown used to a horizontal position. I became nauseous each time they raised me into a vertical position. Days passed before I was used to that position enough to take my first step.

I didn't really learn to walk until after the hospital discharged me. A physical therapist came in every other day to help me. Six months would pass before I learned to walk on my own more than a few steps.

My doctor removed the Ilizarov device eleven and a half months after the accident. After that, I could use a walker and eventually a cane. I walked with leg braces and a cane for a year and a half after the accident.

My accident occurred in January 1989. They removed the external metalwork from my arm fixator in May, but they put internal metal plates down both of the bones of the forearm. Those metal plates stayed there for several more months.

In late November, they removed the fixator from my leg, but that wasn't the end. After that, I remained in a cast for a long time, and they inserted a plate in my leg— which stayed there for nine years. I was content to leave it there, but they said they had to take it out. My doctor explained that the bones would become brittle.

During those years with the fixator and the metal plates, whenever I had to fly, I set off metal detectors from Ohio to California. I would say to the security people, "I have

more stainless steel in me than your silverware drawer at home."

But all these rods and wires and plates worked. People gasped when they saw them embedded in my flesh. Those same people are now awed at my mobility.

9
ENDLESS ADJUSTMENTS

After the ICU, I stayed in the hospital 105 days.

During the months of my recovery, the church worked hard to make me feel useful. They brought vanloads of kids to the hospital to see me. Sometimes committees met in my hospital room. They knew I couldn't say or do much, but it was their way to encourage me. They did everything they could to make me feel worthwhile and useful.

But I had another problem: I didn't want anybody to do anything for me. That's my nature.

One day Jay B. Perkins, a retired minister, came to visit me. He had become a powerful father figure in the ministry for me.

Jay visited me faithfully. He came often to see me, some-times two or three times a week. I wasn't fit company, but I smiled each time anyway. I'd lie in bed and feel sorry for myself. He'd speak kindly, always trying to find words to encourage me, but nothing he said helped—although that wasn't his fault. Not only was I miserable, but as I learned later, I made everyone else miserable.

My visitors tried to help me, and many wanted to do whatever they could for me.

"Can I get you a magazine?" someone would ask.

"Would you like a milkshake? There's a McDonald's in the lobby. Or I could get you a hamburger or . . . ?"

"Would you like me to read the Bible to you? Or maybe some other book?"

"Are there any errands I can run for you?"

My answer was always the same: "No thanks."

I don't think I was mean. I didn't want to see anyone. I didn't want to talk to anyone. I wanted my pain to go away.

Jay noticed how detached I was from friends and family. One day he was sitting beside me when one of the South Park deacons came for a visit. After ten minutes, the man got up and said, "I just wanted to come by and check on you." Then he asked, "Is there anything I can get for you before I leave?"

"Thank you, no. I appreciate it, but—"

"Well, can I get you something to eat? Can I go down-stairs and—"

"No, really. Thanks for coming."

He said good-bye and left.

Jay sat and stared out the window for several minutes after the deacon left. Finally he walked over to the bed and got close to my face and said, "You really need to get your act together."

"Sir?" I said like anyone would say respectfully to an eighty-year-old preacher.

"You need to get your act together," he repeated. "You're not doing a very good job."

"I don't understand what—"

He moved even closer so that I couldn't look away. "These people care about you so much, and you can't imagine how deeply they love you."

"I know they love me."

"Really? Well, you're not doing a very good job of letting them know you're aware. You're not treating them right. They can't heal you. If they could heal you, they would do it. If they could change places with you, many of them would. If you ask them to do anything—anything— they would do it without hesitating."

"I know—"

"But you won't let them do anything for you."

"I don't *want* them to do anything." Without holding anything back, I said as loudly as I could, "The truth is, I don't even want them to be here. I'd just as soon they didn't come. They must have better things to do. I know

that. Why would I want anybody to come and see me like this? It's just awful. I'm pathetic."

"It's not your call."

I stared back, shocked at his words.

"You've spent the better part of your life trying to minister to other people, to help them during times of difficulty and tragedy and—"

"I . . . I've tried to—"

"And now you're doing a terrible job of letting these people do the same thing for you." I'll never forget his next sentence. *Don, it's the only thing they have to offer you, and you're taking that gift away from them.*

His words stunned me. In my thinking, I was trying to be selfless and not cause people any trouble. In reality, I was being selfish.

Jay didn't let up on me. "I want you to let them help you. Did you hear me? You will allow them to help!"

"I can't—I just can't let—"

"Okay, Don, then if you don't do it for yourself, do this for *me*," he said.

He knew I'd do anything for him, so I nodded.

"The next time anyone comes in here and offers to do something—anything, no matter what it is—I want you to say yes. You probably can't do that with everyone, but you can start with just one or two people. Let a few of the people express their love by helping you. Promise me you'll do that."

"I'm not sure I can."

"Yes, you can."

"I'll try, but that's just not me."

"Then make it you." His gaze bored into me. "Do it!" His voice softened. "Just try it for me, would you? You have to get better at this. Right now you're not doing very well. This is one of the lessons God wants you to learn."

"Okay," I said, unable to resist any longer. I promised I would honor his request and do as he asked. I didn't think he would leave until I did.

Two days passed, and I still couldn't do what he asked.

On the third day, a church member popped into my room, greeted me, and spent about five minutes with me before he got up to leave. "I just wanted to come by and check on you and see how you were doing," he said. "You're looking good."

I smiled. I looked terrible, but I didn't argue with him.

He stood up to leave. "Is there anything I can do for you before I go?"

I had my mouth poised to say the words, "No thank you," and an image of Jay popped into my mind. "Well, I wish I had a magazine to read."

"You do?" He had the biggest grin on his face. "Really?"

"I think so. I haven't read one in a while—"

"I'll be right back!" Before I could tell him what kind, he dashed out the door so fast it was like a human blur.

He had to go down twenty-one floors, but it seemed as if he were gone less than a minute. When he returned, he had an armload of magazines. He was still grinning as he showed me the covers of all of them.

I thanked him. "I'll read them a little later," I said.

He put them on the table. "Is there anything else?"

"No, no, that's all I need. Thank you."

Once I had opened the door and allowed someone to do something kind for me, I realized it wasn't so hard after all. After he left, I began skimming through the magazines. I kept thinking about what had happened.

Jay was right.

About forty minutes later, a woman from the singles group came to see me, and we went through the regular ritual of chatting. "How are you doing?"

"Fine."

"Well, can I get you anything?"

"No, I . . . I . . ." Again, Jay's words popped into my head. "Well, maybe a strawberry milkshake."

"Strawberry milkshake? I'd love to get one for you." I don't think I had ever seen her smile so beautifully before. "Anything else? Some fries, maybe?"

"No."

She dashed out the door and came back with a strawberry milkshake. "Oh, Pastor, I hope you enjoy this."

"I will," I said. "As a matter of fact, I love strawberry milkshakes."

Just then I realized how badly I had missed the whole idea. I had failed my visitors and myself. In trying to be strong for them, I had cheated them out of opportunities to strengthen me. Guilt overwhelmed me, because I could—at last—see their gifts to me.

I had learned a lesson.

✝

Someone brought a plaque to me in the hospital. At first, I thought it was supposed to be some kind of joke because it contained the words of Psalm 46:10: "Be still, and know that I am God." Perhaps it was meant to console me. I'm not sure the person who gave it to me (and I don't remember who it was) realized that I couldn't do anything *but* be still.

Yet that plaque contained the message I needed; it just took me a long time to understand that.

Weeks lapsed before I realized that part of what I needed was to be still—inwardly—and to trust that God knew what he was doing through all of this. Yes, it was a verse for me, even though it wasn't one I would have chosen.

God forced me to be still. I had no choice. The longer I lay immobile, the more open I became to God's quietness and to inner silence.

Day after day I lay in bed, unable to move. I lay on my back a total of thirteen months before I could turn over on my side. Just that simple action made it one of the

best days of recovery. "Oh, I had forgotten how good this feels," I said aloud.

During that long recovery, I learned a lot about myself, my attitude, and my nature. I didn't like many things I saw in Don Piper.

Though I know I wasn't the easiest of patients, the nurses of the orthopedic floor treated me with kindness and compassion. I learned to care a great deal for them and admire their dedication. I guess they must have seen something in me as well.

Many months passed, but one day I did walk back into that hospital and hug all those nurses.

But the sweetest moment came when I was discharged from my 105-day stay at St. Luke's. The nurses from my floor all accompanied me down the elevator and to my waiting ambulance on the day of my discharge.

Being surrounded by nurses who had fed me, medicated me, bathed me, and done only the Lord knows what else, made my going home that day so wonderful. It was as if they were saying, "We've done our best. Now you've got to get better and come back and see us."

I can only imagine how different I must have seemed to them that going-home day from the day I had arrived wavering between life and death.

10 BACK TO CHURCH

After I came home from the hospital in the middle of May, I still had to sleep in a hospital bed until February—a total of thirteen months.

My twin sons, Joe and Christopher, were only eight at the time of the accident, and my daughter, Nicole, was twelve. One of the things that hurt me most was the pain my children had to cope with. They didn't say a great deal, but I knew how they felt.

This is a handmade card from Joe, written to me while he was living with his grandparents. (I didn't correct the spelling.)

hi dad,
 You are the best. I love you and I hope you like the cards. I whish this never hapined
 I love you Dad,
 Joe

After I came home from the hospital, most afternoons Joe's twin, Chris, came in from school and into the living room where my bed was. Without saying a word, Chris would walk over and lay his head on my chest. I don't know how long his head lay there, probably not more than a full minute.

He never said a word. He didn't need to. That simple gesture was enough. I felt so loved by my son.

After a minute or so, Chris would go into his room, get out of his school clothes, change into his play clothes, and then go outside and play. That's the way he greeted me almost every day.

As for Nicole, just six months after the accident, I was able to participate in a very special moment for her.

Southern Baptists have mission organizations for young people. The most well-known are the Royal Ambassadors for boys and Girls in Action (GAs) and Acteens for girls. As soon as she was old enough, Nicole participated in GAs and Acteens. When she was fourteen, she learned she would be awarded the honor of Queen with Scepter. This coronation award is presented during a church ceremony.

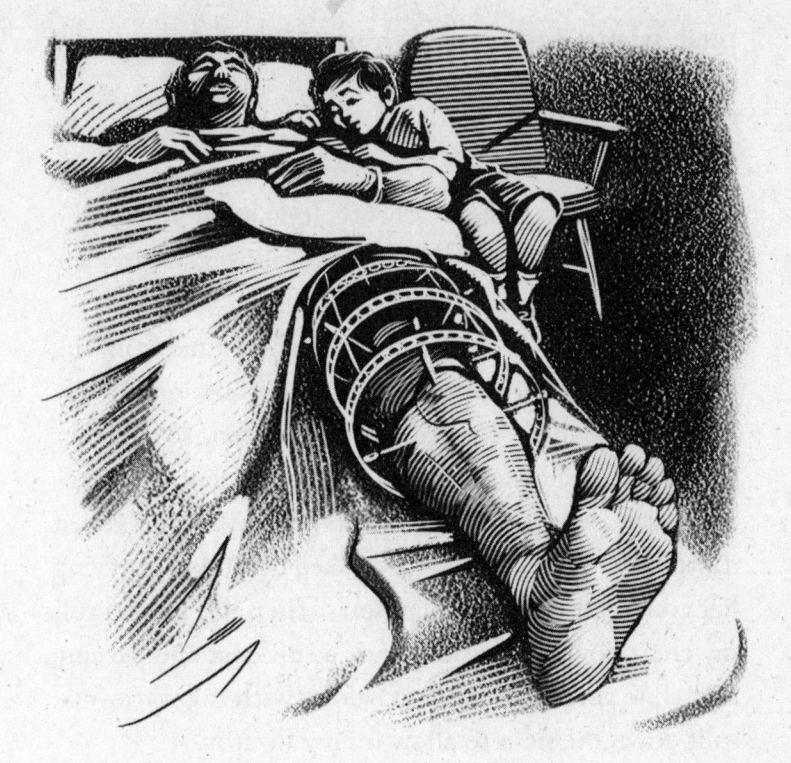

Her receiving the award was a tribute to her own determination. During the time she threw herself into those
activities, she wasn't able to live at home. Our friends
Suzan and Stan Mauldin had opened their home to her,
and she lived with them.

Nicole received no support from me, because I was
barely surviving in the hospital. She received little support from her mother, because Eva's life consisted of
leaving school every afternoon and rushing to the hos-

pital, where she stayed with me until she went home to bed.

The challenges made us all the more proud of Nicole.

One of the traditions associated with the coronation ceremony is that fathers escort their daughters down the aisle. Brothers (if the girls have any) follow and carry the crown and scepter.

I'm grateful that my doctors discharged me from the hospital in time to be present for the coronation. I really wanted to be there. This was the biggest thing so far in her young life, and I wanted to share the moment with her.

I was in a wheelchair, and Nicole held my arm as I rolled down the aisle. Chris and Joe walked behind us, carrying her crown and scepter on pillows. They also helped roll my chair down the aisle. I wore a suit coat and tie (my first time since the accident) along with my warm-ups split down the sides to allow for my Ilizarov.

Not only was Nicole absolutely excited that her daddy could be present for her important occasion, she was thrilled that her father could "walk" her down the aisle.

Tears filled my eyes as I maneuvered down the aisle. I heard others sniffling. But I also knew that we wept tears of joy over this wonderful moment in Nicole's life.

✝

The doctors sent me home initially, I believe, because they thought I'd recover faster in an environment with

family around me. It may also have cost a lot less for me to be home. I'm not sure, but I was glad to be out of the hospital.

Being in my own home wasn't much easier for me or my family, especially Eva. Our living room looked like a hospital room.

But just being around familiar things lifted my spirits. I enjoyed being able to look out the window at my neighborhood and having people who didn't wear white uniforms drop in to see me.

The medical team sent my bed and a trapeze contraption, just like what I had used at the hospital. Nurses visited every day. Physical therapists came every other day.

Some of the sweetest memories I have are of the kind people who simply spent each day with me while Eva went back to work. When church members heard that she had to return to teaching or lose her job, they decided to do what they could.

Ginny Foster, the senior pastor's wife, organized a group of people to stay with me each day. Ginny organized what she laughingly called the "Don Patrol"—mostly women from the church, along with a few retired men.

It was about seven hours from the time Eva left in the morning until she returned. I would generally go to sleep about two or three o'clock in the morning and wake up around ten. The Don Patrol arrived about nine o'clock

while I was still asleep. They either prepared lunch for me or brought it with them.

Often I would awake to find a charming woman knitting at the end of my bed. Or perhaps an older man would be reading the *Houston Chronicle*. He'd lower the newspaper and grin at me. "Good morning. Do you need anything?"

The parade of sweet faces changed every day. Although the volunteers were different, the goals remained the same: take care of Don and keep him company.

As I lay in bed day after day, I realized how much others had done for us. While I was still hospitalized, friends from church had packed up our furniture and moved us to a new house, where I could be on the ground level with no stairs to worry about.

During the day, I would look through the patio window from my "hospital room." Often I spotted high schoolers Brandon and Matt Mealer and their buddy Chris Alston mowing our lawn. One night Chris arranged to borrow our van and surprise me by taking me to a movie. I don't even remember what the movie was, but I will never forget his thoughtfulness. Once when our fence blew down during a windstorm, it was back up before we could call anyone to help.

For months after I came home, good-hearted members of the Don Patrol transported me back and forth for water therapy. I wasn't out of the bed for more than probably

five minutes a day except for therapy. Some days I didn't even get out of bed.

The worst part is that once I was in the hospital bed, I was completely incapacitated. I couldn't get up or do anything for myself. Without the help of the therapist, I never would have sat up or been able to move on my own again.

Slowly, gradually, I learned to walk again. The first day I got out of bed on my own, I took three steps. I slumped back onto the bed, exhausted. But I smiled. *I had walked.* Three steps sounds like so little, and yet I felt a powerful sense of accomplishment.

"I did it!" I shouted to the silent room. "I walked! I walked!"

Walking again was a reminder of what we all take for granted every day as we talk, move, and live. For a long time, taking just three shaky steps seemed like climbing Mount Everest.

Taking those first steps at home on my own remains one of the best moments of my recovery. Those few steps convinced me that I was getting better. Now I had goals to work toward. I had gone through the worst part of the recovery. I knew I would continue to improve. Each day I took a few more steps. By the end of the week, I had made a complete circle of the living room.

When Eva came home and watched me demonstrate my daily progress, her smile made me feel as if I had won

a marathon. She reacted with joyful delight the afternoon I showed her that I could walk throughout the house all by myself.

✝

A week after I came home from the hospital, I had decided I wanted to go to church on a Sunday morning. With the help of a small group, we planned for them to help me get there. In case I couldn't make it, we didn't want to disappoint anyone, so we decided not to announce it to the congregation.

By then I could sit in a wheelchair—as long as some-one was there to lift me out of bed and into it—but I still couldn't stand up. Six friends from church came to our house and took the seats out of one of the church vans. At the church, they had constructed a ramp so they could roll me up to its doors.

I kept thinking of all the work I had laid on them. Several times I started to apologize, but they assured me it was their pleasure.

Then I remembered Jay's words. My family and friends saw me the first day of the accident. I never saw what I looked like. They endured the shock and the fear. In some respects, this ordeal was more difficult for my family and friends than it was for me. They loved being able to help me. In a way, this was part of their own recovery, and they were glad to be able to do something special for me.

It was still hard to let them do everything for me. I felt totally helpless and absolutely dependent on them. As I realized that once again, I smiled.

"Thank you," I said, then allowed them to take care of me.

They carefully put me into the van, drove me to the church, and pulled up at the side door. When one of the men in the van opened the door, church members on their way into the sanctuary saw me.

"Look! It's Pastor Don!" someone yelled.

I heard cheering and clapping as people stood around and made way for the men to wheel me up the ramp.

People rushed toward me. It seemed as if everyone wanted to touch me or shake my hand. I could hardly believe the fuss they made over me.

Finally someone wheeled me inside and stopped my chair in front of the platform near the church organ. It wasn't possible to lift me up.

By then the entire congregation had become aware that I was in front of the sanctuary. I smiled as I thought, *It's taken me five months to get back to church. I may be slow, but I'm faithful.*

Just then someone whispered in my ear, "We want you to say something to the congregation." He got behind me and steered me toward the center of the sanctuary, right in front of the pulpit.

I became completely overwhelmed at the congregation's loving response. I didn't know if I could speak. What could I say after all those weeks of absence and all I'd been through?

Someone thrust a microphone in my hand. Then applause broke out. Every person in that building stood, and the applause began—and it kept on for a long time. I finally waved for them to stop.

Just then God spoke to me. This was one of the few times in my life when I heard a very clear voice inside my head.

They're not applauding for you.

It made a difference, and I could speak. Finally, I had it straight. They were giving thanks to God for what he had done for me. God had brought me back from death to life once again. I relaxed. This was a moment to glorify God. This wasn't praise for me.

I still had to wait for what seemed like a long time until the applause ceased. I spoke only four words. Anyone who was there that glorious day can tell you what they were: "You prayed. I'm here."

The congregation erupted in applause again. If I had said anything else, I'm sure they wouldn't have heard it anyway.

I couldn't say it, but I believed then—and still do—that I survived only because a number of people wanted me

to. They believed God would hear them. People prayed for me who had never seriously prayed before.

When I did live, those same people—especially those who hadn't been in the habit of praying—said the experience changed their lives. In some instances, individuals I had never met—from Cottonwood, Arizona, to Buffalo, New York—heard my story second-, third-, and fourth-hand.

Over the next three years, people would approach me and say, "I saw you on a video interview. You're the man! I prayed for you." Or they heard one of the audiotapes of my testimony distributed by my church and would say, "You just don't know what it means. God heard *our* prayers, and we're so happy you lived."

To some individuals, I'm not really a person but a symbol. For them, I represent answered prayer. They pleaded for me to survive, and I did. I don't know what to make of it, except to say that this is something outside of and beyond me.

Since I began to tell others about my experience in heaven, I can't begin to count the people who have come to me and asked such questions as, "Is heaven real?" "What is heaven really like?" Or they'll ask specific questions about the praise or the streets of gold. Someone seems to always mention a recently departed loved one.

Just to know that I've been there and come back to earth and am able to talk to them seems to bring deep comfort to many. Sometimes it amazes me.

Others look at the marks on my body even today and say, "You're a miracle because of all you went through. You're a walking miracle."

11 OPENING UP

God used my closest friend, David Gentiles, to keep me alive, and I'm grateful. He also used David again in my life nearly two years after the accident.

Until then I had never talked to anyone about my heavenly experience. In a general sense, I had talked to Eva, but I always closed off the conversation before she asked questions. To her credit, she never pressured me to say anything more. It wasn't that I wanted to withhold anything from Eva; I just couldn't talk about the experience.

Nearly a year and a half after my release from the hospital, David came to the house to spend time with me.

When the two of us were alone, I had a flashback to the time when I had been lying in ICU and had told him

I couldn't go on. That's when he had told me he would pray me through. We talked about that day, and I thanked him again for his friendship and prayer.

"How are you feeling now?" he asked.

"I'm in pain." I tried to laugh and added, "I'm always in pain, but that's not the worst part for me right now."

He leaned closer. "What is the worst part?"

"I just don't know where I'm going. I lack any clear direction about my future."

David listened as I talked about the things I would like to do, the things I couldn't physically do, and how I wasn't sure that God wanted me to continue at the church. I felt loved and needed there, but I wasn't sure that was where I should be.

He listened for a long time and then asked gently, "What did you learn from your accident and recovery experience?"

For three or four minutes I shared several things, especially about letting other people inside and allowing them to help me. Then I said, "But in the midst of all this suffering and despair, I have learned that heaven is real."

He raised his eyebrows. "What do you mean by that?"

Slowly, hesitantly, I shared a little—very little—about my brief visit to heaven.

"Tell me more," he said, and I didn't hear it as prying. He was my friend and wanted to know. I also sensed that

I could speak about heaven to David and that he would understand, as much as any human being was able to.

"I died in that accident. The next moment I stood in heaven," I said.

He leaned forward, and I saw the excitement in his eyes.

After I had shared my experience in heaven, he said nothing, and a peaceful silence filled the room. Our friendship was such that we didn't have to fill the gap with words.

David finally nodded slowly and asked, "Why haven't you talked about this before?"

"I have two very good reasons. Number one, if I go around talking about having been in heaven, people will think I'm nuts."

"Why would you think that? I heard you, and I didn't—"

"Number two," I said, interrupting him, "I don't want to go over that experience again. It's . . . well, it's just too personal. Too special. It's not that I don't want to share it, but I don't think I can."

"Why do you think you experienced heaven if you're not supposed to share it?"

"I'll tell you a better question I've asked myself—why did I experience it and have it taken away from me? What was that all about?" Months of pent-up anger poured out. "And why did I have to go through this? I saw the glory and the beauty—the most powerful, overwhelming expe-

rience in my life—and then I had to come back. Why? For this?" I pointed to my arm and leg. "I was in an accident that took my life. Immediately I went to heaven, and it was greater and more wonderful than anything I've ever imagined. And then I was pulled back to this life again. My body is a mess. I'm constantly in pain. I'll never be healthy or strong again."

David stared at me and asked again, "Why do you think you experienced heaven if you're not supposed to share it?"

"I don't have an answer for that question."

"Is it possible that God took you to heaven and brought you back for you to share what happened to you? Don't you realize what a powerful encouragement you can be to others?"

His words shocked me. I had been so focused on myself, I hadn't thought about anyone else. I tried to relate to him how I felt. I cried in his presence, and I knew it was all right.

For perhaps twenty minutes we discussed sharing my experience. David nudged me, and although I knew he was right, it still wasn't easy for me to do.

Finally David said, "I want you to make a covenant with me."

"What kind of covenant?"

"Simple. Pick two people you trust. Just tell them a little of your experience and gauge their response." He

went on to explain that if they thought I was crazy, then I would never have to speak about it again.

"But if they rejoice with you," he said, "and if they urge you to tell them more, I want you to take this as a sign—a sign that God wants you to talk about those ninety minutes you spent in heaven."

After considering the matter carefully, I covenanted with him. "I can do that much."

"When?"

"I promise to do it soon."

"Very soon, right?"

"Okay, I promise I won't put it off."

David prayed for me, and as I listened to him speak, the certainty came over me. It was no longer a choice—I had to speak out.

First, I decided on those I could trust with my holy secret. Once I had narrowed it down to a handful, I made sure it was a one-on-one conversation. I'd wait until the matter of my health came up—and it always did—and then I'd say something simple such as, "You know, I died that day. And I woke up in heaven."

The reaction was the same each time: "Tell me more." They didn't always say those words, but that's what they wanted. I could see their eyes widen, and they wanted to know more.

As I shared a little more, no one questioned my sanity.

"You have to tell people about this," one friend said.

"That experience wasn't just for you," another said. "It's for us as well. It's for me."

As I listened to each one over the next two weeks, I realized I was right back where I had been in the hospital the time Jay had rebuked me. That time I wouldn't let anyone help me, and it was selfish. This time I wouldn't share what had happened to me—and it was also selfish.

Okay, I'll talk about it, I vowed to myself.

Since virtually everyone already knew about my auto accident, I used the occasion as the natural catalyst to speak about my time in heaven—cautiously at first. As people responded with overwhelming support, I became more open about my story.

Even though I knew it was what I was supposed to do, it wasn't easy for me. Today, I only discuss my glimpse of heaven when someone asks, and then only because I feel that person really wants to know. Otherwise, I still won't talk about it.

That's part of the reason it's taken me so many years to write this book. It was such a personal experience that going back over it repeatedly isn't something I feel comfortable doing.

I talk about my experience both publicly and to individuals. I'm writing about what happened because my story seems to mean so much to people for many different reasons. For example, when I speak to any large

crowd, at least one person will be present who has recently lost a loved one and needs assurance of that person's destination.

When I finish speaking, it still amazes me to see how quickly the line forms of those who want to talk to me. They come with tears in their eyes and grief written all over their faces. I feel so grateful that I can offer them peace and assurance.

I've accepted that my words do bring comfort, but it was never something I thought about doing. If it hadn't been for David Gentiles pushing me, I'm sure that even to this day I wouldn't have told anyone. I'm grateful for his urging me.

My experience has changed many things about the way I look at life. First, I'm thoroughly convinced that God answers prayer. Answered prayer is why I'm still alive.

Second, I have an unquestionable belief that God is in the miracle business. Every day I thank God that I'm a living, walking, talking miracle.

Third, I want as many people as possible to go to heaven. I've always believed heaven is real and a place for God's people. Since my own experience of having been there, I've felt a stronger sense of responsibility to make the way clear. Not only do I want people to go to heaven, I now feel an urgency about helping them give their hearts to Jesus, because I know heaven is real and Jesus is the way to get there.

One time Dick Onerecker and I talked about this. I told him, "Again, Dick, I want to thank you for saving my life. I can't thank you enough for your faithfulness in obeying God that rainy day."

Dick said that hearing about my experience and his role in my coming back to earth had set him free. After that he felt a boldness to talk about Jesus Christ that he hadn't had before.

12
THE CLASPING HAND

I was privileged to share my story in Dick's church a little more than a year after the accident. His wife, Anita, was there, and so was my own family. Because I still wore leg braces, two people had to help me walk up on the platform.

I told everyone about the accident and about Dick's part in bringing me back. "I believe I'm alive today because Dick prayed me back to earth," I said. "In my first moments of consciousness, two things stand out. First, I was singing 'What a Friend We Have in Jesus.' The second was that Dick's hand gripped mine and held it tight."

After the morning worship, many of us went out to lunch together at a Chinese restaurant. Anita sat across from me. I remember sipping my wonton soup and having a delightful time with the church members.

When there was a lull in the conversation, Anita leaned across the table and said in a low voice, "I appreciated everything you said this morning."

"Thank you—"

"There's just one thing—one thing I need to correct about what you said in your message."

"Really?" Her words surprised me. "What did I say that was incorrect?"

"You were talking about Dick getting into the car with you. Then you said he prayed for you while he was holding your hand."

"Yes, I remember that part very distinctly. I have a number of memory gaps, and most of the things I don't remember. The one thing that's totally clear was Dick being in the car and praying with me."

"That's true. He did get in the car and pray with you." She leaned closer. "But, Don, he never held your hand."

"I distinctly remember holding his hand."

"That didn't happen. It was physically impossible."

"But I remember that so clearly. It's one of the most vivid—"

"Think about it. Dick leaned from the rear of the trunk over the backseat and put his hand on your *shoulder* and

touched you. You were facing forward, and your left arm was barely hanging together."

"Yes, that's true."

"Dick said you were slumped over on the seat toward the passenger side."

I closed my eyes, visualizing what she was saying. I nodded.

"Your right hand was on the floor of the passenger side of the car. Although the tarp covered the car, there was enough light for him to see your hand down there. There was no way Dick could have reached your right hand."

"But . . . but . . ." I sputtered.

"Someone was holding your hand. But it wasn't Dick."

"If it wasn't Dick's hand, whose was it?"

She smiled and said, "I think you know."

I put down my spoon and stared at her for several seconds. I had no doubt whatsoever that someone had held my hand. Then I understood. "Yes, I think I know too."

Immediately I thought of the verse in Hebrews about entertaining angels unaware. As I pondered for a moment, I also remembered other incidents where there was nothing but a spiritual explanation. For instance, many times in the hospital room in the middle of the night, I would be at my worst. I never saw or heard anyone, but I felt a presence—something, someone—sustaining and encouraging me. That also was something I hadn't talked

about. I couldn't explain it, so I assumed others wouldn't understand.

This was another miracle, and I wouldn't have known about it if Anita hadn't corrected me.

Dick died of a heart attack in 2001. I confess that I was saddened to hear of his passing but delighted that he is in glory. Dick saved my life, and God took him to heaven first. I was glad he heard me share about my journey to heaven before he made his own trip.

Anita has become a dear family friend, and my testimony about heaven has given her real peace about Dick's being with Jesus. Since that experience with her, I've been more convinced than ever that God brought me back to this earth for a purpose. The angel gripping my hand was God's way of letting me know that he would not let go of me no matter how hard things became.

I may not feel that hand each day, but I know it's there.

13
THE NEW NORMAL

Some things happen to us that we never recover from, and they disrupt our lives. That's how life is. We must forget the old standard and accept a "new normal."

I wasted a lot of time thinking about how I used to be healthy and had no physical limitations. In my mind, I'd reconstruct how life *should* be, but in reality, I knew my life would never be the same. I had to adjust and accept my physical limits as part of my new normal.

As a child, I'd sit on a big brown rug in my great-grandparents' living room and listen to them talk about the good old days. After hearing several stories, I thought the

recollections they shared didn't seem so great. Maybe for them they truly were.

At some points in our lives, most of us want to go back to a happier time. We can't, but we still keep dreaming about how it once was.

In my twenties, I was a radio disc jockey. We used to play oldies, and people who called in to request those songs often commented that music used to be better than it is now.

The reality is that in the old days we played good and bad records, but the bad ones faded from memory just like bad ones do now. No one ever asked us to play the music that bombed. The good songs make the former times seem great, as if all the music was outstanding. But there was bad music thirty years ago or fifty years ago—in fact, a lot of bad music.

The same is true with experiences. We forget the negative and go back to recapture pleasant events.

Once that idea got through to me, I decided I couldn't recapture the past. That part of my life was over, and I would never be healthy or strong again. The only thing for me to do was to discover a new normal.

Yes, I said to myself, *there are things I will never be able to do again. I don't like that and may even hate it, but that doesn't change the way things are. The sooner I accept the way things are, the sooner I'll be able to live in peace and enjoy my new normal.*

Here's an example of what I mean.

In early 2000, I took a group of college kids on a ski trip from Houston to Colorado. Skiing is one of the things I'd always loved doing. Unable to participate, I sat in a clubhouse at the bottom of the hill, gazed out the window, and watched them glide down. Sadness came over me, and I thought, *I made a big mistake. I should never have come here.* As happy as I was for them, I mourned over my inability ever to ski again.

Then I thought for the thousandth time of other things I would never do again. When I was a senior pastor, most of the adults had greeted me at the door following each morning service. "Enjoyed your sermon," they'd said. "Great service."

Kids, however, behaved differently. They'd race up with a picture they'd colored for me. Before my accident, I loved the kids flocking around me. I'd kneel down and talk with them. After my recovery, I couldn't squat down and stare at their smiling faces the way I used to before as I said, "Thank you very much. I really like this picture. This is very nice."

After my accident, the best I could do was lean forward and talk to them. Perhaps that doesn't seem like a big thing, but it is for me. I'll never squat again. I'll never be able to kneel so that I can be at a child's level again, because my legs won't give me the ability to do that.

Sometimes things we take for granted every day can be taken from us suddenly, and we're changed forever.

✝

During my long hospitalization, somebody gave me a magazine article about a young man who lost his sight. He went through a bitter time. A friend who cared enough about him to tell him the truth said, "You need to get past this. I want you to make a list of all the stuff you can still do."

"Now what kind of a list would that be?" the angry blind man asked.

"Just do it for me. Make a list of all the things you can still do. And I'm talking about simple things like 'I can still smell flowers.' Make the list as extensive as you can. When you're finished, I want to hear that list."

The blind man finally agreed and made the list. I don't know how much time passed, but when the friend returned, the blind man was smiling and peaceful.

"You seem like you're in a much better frame of mind than the last time I saw you," the friend said.

"I am. I really am, and that's because I've been working on my list."

"How many things are on your list?"

"About a thousand so far."

"That's fantastic."

"Some of them are very simple. None of them are big, but there are thousands of things I can still do."

The blind man had changed so radically that his friend asked, "Tell me what made you change."

"I've decided to do all the stuff I can. The more I thought about it, the fewer limitations I saw. There are thousands of things I can do—and I'm going to do them for the rest of my life."

After I read that article, I thought, *That's exactly what I need—not going back over the way things used to be or what I used to have that I don't have anymore. I need to discover what I have now, not only to celebrate but also to recognize I'm not helpless.*

In the article, the blind man said something like, "I'm not going to worry about what I can't do. I'm going to do what I can do well." Those words seemed simple.

I read that article at just the right time. God had sent the message I needed when I needed it.

It was one of those powerful moments that caused me to say, "I've got to get on with my life. Whatever I have, I'm going to use it to the max."

✝

During the 105 days I spent in the hospital, Eva had the most strain. She got up at 6:00 every morning, did everything she had to do around the house, and hurried to school to teach. As soon as school was over, she rushed to my bedside, where she stayed until 10:30 every night. Day after day it was the same stressful routine.

One of the most challenging experiences for her—by herself—was to buy a van to replace my wrecked car. By then, I was home and able to walk with my Ilizarov still attached. That meant, however, that if I wanted to go anywhere, we had to have a van to transport me. We had no idea how long it would be before I could sit in a regular car.

Eva had never bought a vehicle in her life, but she went to a dealer, test-drove a van, picked one out, and brought it home. "Here's our van," she said.

She made me proud of her—and I felt very grateful.

I learned to drive again in that van. One day as the family was washing it, I walked outside still wearing my Ilizarov. As I lumbered around the van, I noticed that the driver's side door was open. Peering inside, I calculated what it would take for me and my thirty pounds of stainless steel to get behind the wheel. While the family wasn't looking, I maneuvered myself into the seat and started the engine. My family was stunned.

Eva came around to the door and asked, "What are you doing?"

I smiled and said, "I'm going for a drive!"

She stammered, "But you can't."

However, something told me that it was now or never for taking the wheel and driving again.

I backed out slowly and drove around the block. It wasn't a long drive, but it was another milestone in my recovery. I'm still not very fond of eighteen-wheelers or

long two-lane bridges, but so far I manage to get where I'm going.

Of course, it fell on Eva to make all my appointments and to see that I got to my doctor's office twice a week. And I must add that I wasn't the easiest person to look after. In fact, I was difficult. As my health improved, I became demanding and curt (I wasn't aware of that), and Eva agonized over trying to please me, although she handled it well.

The fact is that I was very unhappy. Many of my problems stemmed from my feeling completely helpless. For a long time I couldn't even get myself a glass of water. Even if I could have poured one for myself, I couldn't have drunk it without help. Even the simplest tasks made me feel useless.

Eva often had to make decisions on the spot without talking to me. She did the best she could. At times, when she related what she had done, I was quick to let her know how I would have done it. Almost immediately, I'd realize I hurt her feelings when I did that, but the words had been said. I reminded myself, and her, "I'm sorry. You're doing the best you can." I also reminded myself that regardless of how I would have done things, I wasn't able to do them. I just wish I had been a better patient and made it easier for her.

But the worst part of my convalescence for the family was that we farmed out our three kids. They lived with other people for about six months. Our twin sons stayed with Eva's parents in Louisiana. I know they weren't happy about having to move so far away, but they handled it quite well. They were still in elementary school, and at that age, it probably wasn't too difficult relocating.

Nicole, who was five years older and thirteen at this time, moved in with a girlfriend's family and was able to stay in her middle school.

The accident happened in January, and the kids didn't come home permanently until June. They came to see me on weekends during my hospital stays, which was tough on them. When they made their first visit to the hospital, a staff psychologist took all three kids into a room and showed them a life-size dummy with devices attached to it, similar to what was on my body. This way he could explain what they would see when they entered my room. I'm glad he did that, because even many adults, not having that kind of preparation, showed obvious shock when they first saw me.

When the children came into my room the first time, all three of them stepped as close as they could to hug me. They loved me and wanted to see for themselves that I was okay. It did me a lot of good just to see them. The staff didn't let them stay long.

As awful as I looked, the children believed me when I said I would get well. My kids were probably more confident about my recovery than I was.

Although they don't admit it, there probably is a "Dad gap" for my children, especially the twins. Because they were eight years old, they missed my being there to help them learn to do things such as play team sports and go camping.

Looking back, I think the accident affected my parents more permanently than anybody. They were devastated. I'm the oldest of three sons, and all of us had been healthy.

Then, suddenly, when I reached the age of thirty-eight, they were heartbroken and felt helpless to do anything for me. For a long time, they thought I would probably die.

When they came to see me during the first week in the hospital, Mom fainted. Dad grabbed her and helped her out of the room. She wasn't prepared to see me in such bad shape. I'm not sure anyone would have been.

I remember a private moment I had with my father one day. Mom had stepped out of the room. Alone now, my father came close to my bed and took my only unbroken limb, my right hand, in his gnarled hand. He leaned close to me and with great emotion and absolute honesty said, "I would give anything to trade places with you and take this on me."

More than at any other time, I realized how much my dad loves me.

✝

Repeatedly, my doctor told me, "Everything we did for you is the best we can do. Don't count on being able to live a long, productive life. Because of arthritis and a lot of other complications that will set in, you're going to have an uphill battle to be even as mobile as you are now."

He knew what he was talking about. I've felt the beginning of arthritis. Weather changes affect me. I grow tired faster. I think it's a reflection of the fact that I have

to use my legs and knees in ways God didn't design them to be used.

Even today, if someone comes from behind and slaps me on the back, I have to catch myself or I'll keep going forward. I can't lock my knee into place to keep from losing my balance and pitching forward.

I've tried to make light of this, quipping, "I've fallen in some of the best places in Texas." Or, "I've considered commissioning some little plaques that say, 'Don Piper fell here.'"

Despite everything the doctors did for me, one of my legs is an inch and a half shorter than the other. That alone makes my backbone curve. My backbone is beginning to show wear and tear, as are my hip joints.

My left elbow is so messed up I can't straighten it out. Doctors did everything they could, including operating on it several times. The elbow was fractured on the inside, and when it knitted back together, it wouldn't allow me to straighten it. To use the doctor's expression, "It's a very gimpy joint."

This is part of my new normal.

✝

Once after a visit to Dr. Tom Greider's office, he asked me back into his private suite. We talked about a lot of things.

On a whim I asked, "Tom, just how bad was I when they brought me in that night of the accident?"

He didn't flinch. "I've seen worse." He paused for a moment, leaned over his desk, and then continued, "But none of them lived."

I've had to find different ways to do things. I am alive, however, and I intend to serve Jesus Christ as long as I remain alive. But I already know what's ahead, waiting for me.

I'm ready to leave this earth anytime.

14 TOUCHING LIVES

Sometimes I still ask God why I wasn't allowed to stay in heaven. I have no answer to that question. I have learned, however, that God brings people into my life who need to hear my message, giving me the opportunity to touch their lives.

One of the first times I was able to minister to someone as a result of my accident was when I was the guest preacher in a large church. I was invited specifically to talk about my trip to heaven. A woman who sat near the front and to my left began to weep shortly after I began to speak. I could see the tears sliding down her cheeks. As soon as we closed the meeting, she rushed up to me and clasped my hand.

"My mother died last week."

"I'm so sorry for your loss—"

"No, no, you don't understand. God sent you here to-night. I needed this kind of reassurance. Not that I didn't believe—I did, but my heart has been so heavy because of the loss. I feel so much better. She *is* in a better place. Oh, Reverend Piper, I needed to hear that tonight." Before I could say anything more, she hugged me and added, "God sent *me* here tonight because I needed this. I'm a believer, but I needed to hear those words. I needed to know about heaven from someone who had been there."

She was the first to talk to me that way, but certainly not the last. I've heard this kind of response hundreds of times. It still amazes me that I can be a blessing to so many just by sharing my experience.

Two years after the accident, when I still wore leg braces and walked with crutches, I took a group of our young people to a conference at Houston's First Baptist Church. Dawson McAllister, a great teacher of youth, was the speaker. He's so popular he fills up the place.

As happens when working with teens, we were late in leaving South Park Church. I didn't say anything, but I felt extremely irritated with the delay. I had wanted to arrive early because I knew the best seats would be taken if we didn't get there at least an hour before starting time.

I tried not to let it show, but I was still upset by the time we reached First Baptist Church. Once we went inside

the huge building, we realized—as I had expected—that all the seats on the lower floor were filled. We'd have to climb the stairs.

I groaned at the thought of having to do more walking. Even though I was mobile, wearing those braces and the pressure of the crutches under my armpits tired me out. To make it worse, the elevator wasn't working. *If that person hadn't been late*, I kept thinking, *I wouldn't have to hobble up all those stairs.*

It wasn't just clumping up the stairs, but the auditorium was so full that the only places left to sit were in the top rows. Our young people raced ahead to claim those seats. They promised to save one for me on the end. I counted 150 steps as I painfully made my way up.

By the time I finally reached the top, exhaustion had overcome me. I could hardly walk the last flight and across the back of the auditorium to the seat the kids had saved for me. Before I sat down—which also demanded a lot of effort—I rested by leaning against the wall. As I tried to catch my breath, I asked myself, *What am I doing here?*

I could have gotten other adults to take the kids, but I really wanted to be with them. I wanted to feel useful again. I also knew this would be an exciting event for the youth, and I wanted to be part of it. Boisterous laughter and shouting back and forth filled the place. The youth were ready to be blessed and challenged, but at that moment, I didn't think about the kids or how much they

would get out of the meeting. I thought only of being worn out.

At that moment, self-pity took over. As I continued to lean against the wall, my gaze swept the auditorium. I spotted a teenage guy in a wheelchair two sections over. He was sitting with his head in his hands, his back to me.

As I stared at him, I *knew* I had to go over and talk to him. Suddenly I didn't question my actions and forgot about being tired.

I leaned my crutches against the wall and then slowly, painfully made my way across to his section and down the steps. He was a large, good-looking kid, maybe sixteen years old.

When I got closer, I realized why I needed to talk to him. He was wearing an Ilizarov frame—which I hadn't been able to see from where I had stood. My tiredness vanished, along with my anger and self-pity. It was as if I saw myself in that wheelchair and reexperienced all the pain of those days.

He was looking away from me when I laid my hand on his shoulder. His head spun around, and he glared at me.

"That really hurts, doesn't it?" I asked.

He looked at me as if to say, *What kind of fool are you?* Instead he said, "Yeah. It hurts very much."

"I know." I patted his shoulder. "Believe me, I know."

His eyes widened. "You do?"

"I do. I had one too."

"It's horrible."

"I know that. It's just horrible. I wore one on my left leg for eleven months."

"Nobody ever understands," he said.

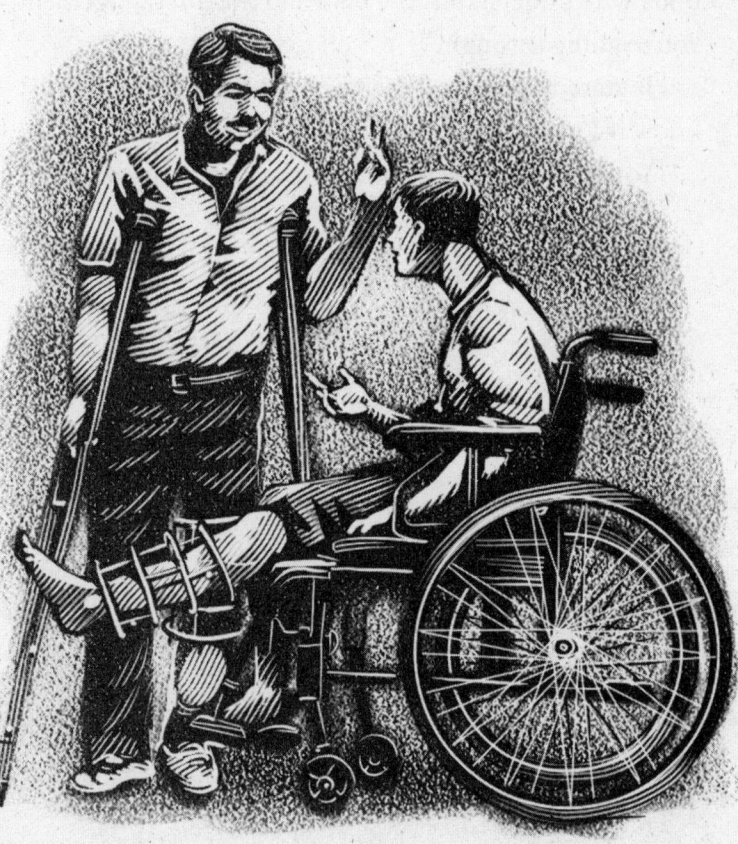

"They can't. It's not something you can talk about and have anyone understand your pain."

For the first time I saw something in his eyes. Maybe it was hope. Maybe it was just a sense of peace because he had found someone who knew what he was going through. We had connected.

"My name is Don," I said, "and you've just met somebody who understands the pain and the discouragement you're going through."

He stared at me, and then his eyes moistened. "I don't know if I'm going to make it."

"You're going to make it. Trust me, you'll make it."

"Maybe," he said.

"What happened?"

"I had a skiing accident."

I noticed that he was wearing a letter jacket. I asked, "You a football player?"

"Yes, sir."

Briefly I told him about my accident, and he told me more about what had happened to him. "I'm going to tell you something," I said. "One day you will walk again."

His face registered skepticism.

"You might not play football again, but you'll walk." I handed him my business card. "My number is on the card, and you can call me anytime, day or night, twenty-four hours a day."

He took the card.

"I'm going to walk back up there to my kids." I pointed to where they sat. "I want you to watch me. And as you watch, I want you to know that one day you will walk too." I laughed. "And I'll bet you'll walk better than I do."

He reached up, grabbed me, and hugged me. He held me tight for a long time. I could feel his constricted breathing as he fought back tears. Finally he released me and mumbled his thanks.

That young man needed somebody who understood. I don't know that I had much to offer, but I had my experience, and I could talk to him about pain. Had I not gone through it myself, I'd just be telling him, "I hope you feel better. You're going to be okay"—well-meaning words that most people used.

When I reached the top row, perspiration drenched my body from all the effort, but I didn't care. I turned around. He still stared at me. I smiled and waved, and he waved back. The despair had left his face.

Over the next six months, I received three calls from him, two just to talk and one late at night when he was really discouraged. They were phone calls I will always cherish.

✝

One time, a Houston TV station scheduled me to appear on a live talk show. While I was waiting to speak, the producer came in and began to explain how the show

worked and some of the questions I could expect to be asked.

"That's fine," I said. "Who else is a guest on the show?"

"You're it."

"Wait a minute. You're going to do an hour-long show and I'm the only guest?"

"That's right."

I wondered what I would talk about for an hour. It was fairly early in my recovery, and at the time I had no idea how interested people were in my story. By then the doctor had removed the Ilizarov frame, and I was wearing braces and using crutches. I had brought pictures of me in the hospital, which they televised that day. And I brought the Ilizarov device itself.

Once the TV interview started, I told my story, and then the host asked me questions. The hour passed quickly. While we were still live on the show, a woman called the TV station and insisted, "I need to talk to Reverend Piper immediately."

They wouldn't interrupt the program, but as soon as the program ended, someone handed me a slip of paper with her telephone number. I called her.

"You've got to talk to my brother," she said.

"What's the matter with him?"

"He was involved in a fight in a bar, and another man pulled out a shotgun and blew his leg off. He's wearing one of those things like you used to have on your leg."

"Of course I'll talk to him," I said. "Where is he?"

"He's home in bed."

"Give me the address and I'll go—"

"Oh no, you can't go over there. He's angry and mean. And he's violent. He won't talk to anybody who comes to see him." She gave me his telephone number. "Please call him, but he's so mean right now, I guarantee that he'll cuss you out." Then she added, "And he may just hang up on you, but try him anyway. Please."

As soon as I got home, I called her brother and introduced myself. Before I had spoken more than three sentences, he did just what she had predicted. He yelled at me. He screamed and let me have it with just about every swear word I'd ever heard, and he repeated them several times.

When he paused I said quietly, "I had one of those things on my leg that you have—that fixator."

He didn't say anything for a few seconds, so I said, "I wore one of those Ilizarov devices on my left leg. I know what you must be going through."

"Oh, man, this is killing me. It hurts all the time. It's just . . ." And he went off again as if he hadn't heard me, expressing his anger with a lot of profanity.

When he paused again, I said, "I understand what it feels like to have one of them."

"You don't have it anymore?"

"No, I finally got it off. If you do what you're supposed to do, you can get yours off one day." That didn't sound like much, but it was the only thing I could think of to say.

"If I had some wrenches I'd take it off right now."

"If you take it off, you might as well cut your leg off, because it's the only thing that's holding your leg on."

"I know that, but it's just killing me. I can't sleep." He went on to tell me how miserable he was and how much he hated everything.

Then something occurred to me, and I interrupted him. "What does your leg look like? Does it seem to be hot near the pinholes? Is it the same color up and down your skin? Are there certain holes that hurt more than others?"

"Yeah, that's right. One of them especially—man, it hurts real bad."

"Is your sister there yet?" When he said she was, I ordered him, "Put her on the phone."

He didn't argue and she picked up the phone. "Thank you," she said. "I appreciate so—"

"Listen to me," I said, interrupting her. "I want you to call an ambulance *right now*. You need to get your brother to the hospital as fast as you can. He has a serious infection in that leg. If he doesn't get there soon, he's going to lose his leg."

"You think so?"

"I'm telling you. He has all the symptoms. He's probably got a fever too. Have you checked?"

"Yes, that's right. He's running a fever."

"Get him to the hospital immediately. Call me after-ward."

The next day she called. "Oh, you were right! He has an infection, and he was in terrible shape. They gave him antibiotics. They said he got there just in time, and he's doing better today."

"I assume he's still in the isolation unit." When she said he was, I added, "I'm going to come see him."

As a minister I could get in to see him. I went to the hospital, talked to him, and prayed with him. Eventually that young man turned to Jesus Christ.

If I hadn't been on that TV show and his sister hadn't watched it, not only might he have lost a leg; there is a strong possibility that he would have died. Not only had God used me to save the young man's physical life, but I had been an instrument in his salvation. That was just one more instance of my beginning to see that God still has things for me to do here on earth.

I had immediately recognized the problem because it had happened to me when I was still in the hospital. I had gotten an infection and began hurting badly. I thought it was just part of the pain I'd have to go through. Then a nurse discovered that I had an infection in one of those pinholes.

I remembered then how days before, one of the nurses apparently had cross-contaminated the pinholes. She was

a surly type and never showed me compassion like the others. She came in and did her work, but she acted as if she resented having to work with me.

The nurses used Q-tips, and they had been instructed to use a new one to clean each hole. I had noticed that this time, the nurse didn't get a fresh Q-tip each time, probably because it was faster not to reach for a new one. I didn't think anything about that until after the hole became infected. My added pain had come about because of her laziness. Once they discovered the infection and my elevated temperature, they rushed me into the isolation unit, where I stayed for two weeks. While I was there, no one could visit me.

Eva complained and told the doctor what happened. I never saw that nurse again, so I don't know if they fired her or transferred her.

✝

As much as I enjoy public speaking, few opportunities excite me more than speaking at my alma mater, Louisiana State University (LSU). My wife and I met at LSU, and two of our three children also studied there.

One of the on-campus organizations where I have spoken on several occasions is the Baptist Collegiate Ministry (BCM). While Nicole was a student at LSU and served as one of the officers in that group, the BCM invited me to speak. Knowing she would be in the audience made the experience even more delightful.

Among the many campus activities the BCM sponsored was a Thursday night praise and worship service called TNT. The committee asked me to speak to them about my accident.

The students advertised my talk all over campus as "Dead Man Talking." Because so many showed up, they scheduled two back-to-back services. As I spoke, the audience seemed mesmerized by the story of a man who died and came back to life. I spoke of heaven, answered prayer, and miracles. I told them about singing "What a Friend We Have in Jesus" in the car with Dick Onerecker.

As each service ended, the praise band led us in a chorus of that meaningful song. I didn't know they were going to do it. While I have no doubt they were led by the Spirit to do so, "What a Friend We Have in Jesus" remains a difficult song for me to hear or sing.

Afterward a large number of students waited around to ask questions. Among them was a student named Walter Foster. He asked many questions himself and listened to the other students' questions as well. When I left the auditorium, Walter followed me. Although I didn't mind, I felt as if he pursued me with dogged determination—as if he couldn't get enough details about heaven or hear enough about my experience.

A few months later, Nicole called me. "Do you remember Walter Foster?" Her voice broke, and she started to cry. As soon as I said I remembered him, she said, "He . . .

he died. He suffered a heart attack! Just like that—and he was gone."

Apparently Walter had known about his serious heart condition and was under medical care. Everyone assumed he was doing all right. Obviously his death shocked all the students who knew him. "Twenty-year-old students aren't supposed to die," one of his friends had said.

After I hung up the phone, I thought back to the day when Walter and I met. The fact that he'd followed me the whole time I was at LSU and plied me with endless questions about heaven caused me to wonder. His questions seemed more than just curiosity. *Maybe*, I thought, *even then God was preparing him for his homeward journey.*

His sudden death devastated his friends, especially those involved with the Baptist Collegiate Ministry. They were a close-knit group and mourned the loss of their dear member. The night following his death, they gathered at the BCM building—the place Walter loved most.

During an emotional meeting that night, a number of his friends spoke at length about how much it had meant to Walter that I had shared my experience about heaven. Many mentioned the excitement he expressed to them over what he had heard. He talked about it for days afterward.

"Several times during the day when Reverend Piper was here," one of them said, "Walter told me, 'One day I know I'm going to be in heaven myself!'"

Pressing church business kept me from being at Walter's memorial service in Baton Rouge. Two special requests from his friends were that the preacher would share the gospel message and that someone would sing one particular song. Of course, it was "What a Friend We Have in Jesus." The audience learned the special significance that hymn held for Walter.

Nicole, a music major at LSU and an excellent soloist, sang the song to the assembled mourners. They responded with both great sadness and glorious hope. Tears flowed, and many smiled peacefully.

After the service, students lingered to talk about how much Walter's unwavering belief in heaven had comforted and encouraged them.

One of the other bright things to emerge from my testimony at the BCM and Walter's later passing was the construction and dedication of a prayer garden at the LSU BCM. That seems appropriate to me, because each time I share my story, I stress the importance of prayer. After all, I'm still alive because of answered prayer.

Like many others whose lives have divinely intersected with mine since my accident and my return from heaven, Walter represents those who will be waiting for me the next time God calls me home.

✝

Sue Fayle's first husband died of cancer. His long passing took a lot out of her. She assumed she would live the rest of her life as a widow.

But her neighbor Charles, also without a spouse, changed that. They were not only neighbors, but in their common sense of loss, they became good friends. As time passed, their friendship evolved into love, and they considered marriage.

Sue had reservations about marrying Charles because he came from what she called a rough-and-tough working-class neighborhood. He had a history of hard drinking, and she said, "I can't live with that."

As their love continued to grow, however, Sue issued one simple condition for marriage: "I won't marry a man who gets drunk."

Charles not only stopped getting drunk, he quit drinking altogether. Now they were ready to talk of marriage.

One day they talked about the death of their spouses, both of whom had died of cancer. "If I'm ever diagnosed with cancer," Charles said, "I'll kill myself." He knew that not only did the person with the disease suffer, but their loved ones went through deep agony as well. "I couldn't put anyone through that ordeal," he said.

They did marry and had a good marriage, and Charles never drank again. Sue had already been active in our church, but after their marriage, Charles also became active.

One day, however, he received the one diagnosis he feared most of all: he had cancer. Now he had to face his deep-seated terror. He was afraid that his diagnosis would put Sue through the same terrible ordeal she had faced before.

He also faced another fear after he received the diagnosis. "I'm terrified of dying," he confessed. Although Charles was a church member and said he believed, he was one of those individuals who doubted his salvation. Sue assured him that while she was dedicated to seeing him through this crisis, she was concerned about his lack of assurance of his salvation. She had heard my testimony about heaven on several occasions and had retold my story to others.

"Can you talk to Charles?" she asked me one day. "Please talk to him about salvation, but also tell him about what life is like after death. I believe that a man-to-man talk with Charles would do a lot for him."

I knew Charles, of course, and I suspected he thought he wasn't good enough for God because of his past. I agreed to talk to him.

Charles and I hit it off right away. He was a great guy and easy to relate to. I made it a point to visit him on a regular basis. Whenever I came, Sue excused herself and stayed out of the room until I was ready to leave.

Though Charles's health deteriorated, he never displayed the least bit of anger or depression. We talked about

how difficult it was to be dependent on others for even the most personal functions—bedpans and bathing.

About the fourth time I visited, Charles finally opened up. "I'm afraid. I want to go to heaven, but I need assurance—I want to be certain that when I die, I'll go to heaven."

As he talked about his life, it was obvious that his experience with God was authentic. As is often the case, for many years before he married Sue, he simply hadn't been a faithful follower of Christ. Several times I reminded him of the verses in the Bible that promise heaven for all believers.

"I know, I know," he said. "Before I was saved, I knew I wouldn't go to heaven. I was going to hell. Now I want to be sure about heaven."

My description of heaven encouraged him. "Yes, yes, that's what I want," he said.

On one visit as he talked, he smiled and said, "I'm ready. I'm at peace. I finally know that I'll go to heaven."

On both of the last two visits I made, Charles said, "Tell me again. Tell me once more what heaven is like."

I told him again, even though he had already heard everything I had to say. It was as if his assurance grew each time I talked about heaven.

On the last day of his life on earth, Charles told Sue, "It's going to be all right. I'm going from pain to peace. Someday we'll be together again."

When Sue called and told me, she added, "He died absolutely without fear."

Charles's calm assurance and acceptance gave Sue peace as she worked through her own grief and loss. She told me that only weeks before Charles's death, he'd said listening to my experience and seeing the positive glow in my life made the difference. "It's settled," he'd said. "I know I'm going to a better place."

As Sue shared her memories of Charles, she laughed and said, "Won't I be the lucky one? I've got two men waiting for me. One day, when my time comes, I'll have one on each arm, former husbands who are also brothers in Christ, and they can escort me down the streets of gold."

✝

When Joe, one of my twins, reached his teens, we decided to look for a used car for him. He wanted a truck, so we searched until we found one he liked, a 1993 Ford Ranger.

The dealer's name was Gary Emmons, and he owned a longtime automobile dealership in our area. Once we settled on the truck Joe wanted, we went inside to make the deal. Mr. Emmons gave us an excellent price, and Joe bought the truck.

Because of that experience, a good relationship formed between Gary Emmons and my family. We bought three or four more cars from him after that.

Gary knew a little about what had happened to me, but no details. He was a race-car driver as well as a car dealer. He seemed fascinated with my story. He had said he'd like to hear the whole story one day, but either he was too busy or I had to rush on.

One day Joe went to the dealership to make a payment. Gary waved him over. "You'll never believe this." The man grinned. "An amazing thing happened yesterday."

"What?"

"I went to check out a car that we had just bought. I got inside the car to do the things I usually do—you know, punch all the buttons to see if everything works, listen to the engine for any defects, check the air conditioner, and see if the radio works. I noticed a tape inside the cassette deck. I pushed the eject button." He paused and smiled. "Bet you'll never guess what was on that tape."

"I have no idea," Joe said.

"It was your dad's story. We had bought the car in an auction, so there was no owner to give the tape back to. I took the tape and listened to it. The only thing I could think of when I heard it was one word—*awesome*."

As I look back, I'm amazed. Gary had wanted to hear my story, but we just had not gotten together.

"What are the odds of my going to an automobile auction with thousands of cars for sale," Gary asked Joe,

"then I sit inside one, push a button, and hear your dad talking?"

For days after that, I think Gary must have told everybody he talked to about my accident.

Of course, that testimony thrilled me. I've also heard many other stories of the way God has used my story.

I had made a tape about my experience and had it duplicated. I must have distributed thousands of them. I also know people took the tape and copied it for their friends. I know people who ordered as many as twenty tapes over a period of months.

That testimonial tape just keeps going on and on. Many people who heard my story duplicated it for people going through physical trauma themselves or those dealing with the loss of a loved one.

I can only conclude that God had a plan for Gary Emmons to hear that tape and made sure he did.

✝

One day while I was walking down the hallway of the church, a woman stopped me. That's not unusual, of course. In fact, my wife jokes that it takes me thirty minutes to walk twenty feet because everyone has something they need to ask me or tell me. Our church has over ten thousand members; that's a lot of folks to get around to.

"Oh, Reverend Piper, I came by just to see you. I want to tell you something that I think you need to hear."

Usually when someone starts out that way, they usually add, "It's for your own good," and it's usually not something I want to hear. Several other people were with me, and I wasn't sure how to react. As I stared at her, however, I sensed an urgency in her face and a deep intensity. I turned to the others and asked, "Would you mind?" They were gracious, of course.

"I'm a registered nurse, and you will never believe what happened," the woman said.

"I've had a lot of unbelievable things happen. Just try me."

"This happened at the hospital. A woman who was very ill and hospitalized was able to hear your tape, and it changed her life."

I had heard that before, but I never minded hearing new stories, so I said, "Tell me more."

"Somebody brought her this tape, and she wasn't a believer. But the person wanted her to listen to the tape anyway. Her friends had tried to talk to her about God. They had given her Bibles, all kinds of books, and pamphlets, but nothing affected her. She said, 'I don't want to talk about God, religion, or salvation.' Even though she was terminally ill, she wasn't open to any message about eternity."

She paused to wipe a tear from her eye before she continued. "Somebody brought her a tape—your tape about your experience in heaven—and asked her if she would

listen to it. The friend didn't press it but said something casual like, 'You might find this helpful. It's about a man who died, went to heaven, and came back to life again.'"

The nurse went on to tell me that the woman said she might listen to it. The friend left. The tape lay on the stand next to the bed, unheard.

The woman's health soon deteriorated so badly that doctors told her daughter that it was only a matter of a week, two at the most. The daughter, who was a believer, desperately wanted her mother to hear the tape of my testimony.

The tape contains two messages. The first side tells of the miracles that had to happen for me to live and the answered prayer that took place for me to live. The second side of the tape tells about what heaven is like. I called it "The Cure for Heart Trouble." That's the part the daughter wanted her mother to listen to.

But the woman refused. "I don't want to listen to all that stuff," she said.

Days went by, and the older woman's condition grew more desperate. The nurse talking to me, who was a Christian, realized what was going on. After she talked with the daughter, the nurse decided to talk to the patient herself about her soul—something she had not done before.

After working her shift, the nurse walked into the room and asked, "May I sit down and talk to you a few minutes?"

The dying woman nodded.

Gently the nurse talked about faith and God's peace and how much of a difference Jesus Christ had made in her own life.

The whole time, the woman said nothing.

The nurse mentioned the tape. "I've heard it, and I think it's something you would like to know. Would you like to listen to the tape?"

The old woman nodded, so the nurse put the tape in the cassette recorder and left.

The next day the dying woman told her daughter and the nurse that she had listened to the tape. "I found it very interesting. I'm seriously thinking about becoming a Christian."

Even though the nurse and the daughter rejoiced, they didn't try to pressure the dying woman. Two days passed before the woman said, "I have become a believer." She told her daughter first and then the nurse. After that, no matter who came into the room to see her, the dying woman would say, "I've become a Christian. I've accepted Jesus Christ as my Savior, and I'm going to heaven."

Within hours after her publicly telling others about her conversion, the woman's condition deteriorated. She drifted in and out of consciousness. The next day when the nurse came on duty, she learned that the old woman had died only minutes earlier.

The nurse told me all of that and then said, "You won't believe what was happening during those final moments while she was dying." Before I could ask, she said, "The tape recorder was on the bed beside her, and her daughter had put in the second side of your tape, where you describe heaven. As her life drifted away, she was listening to your account of what heaven is like. The last thing she heard before she left this world to join God in heaven was a description of heaven."

Tears seeped from the corners of my eyes. "Thank you for telling me. That's great encouragement for me."

As she retold some of the story to those with me, I thanked God for bringing me back to earth. *Oh, God, I do see some purpose in my staying here. Thank you for allowing me to hear this story.*

✝

One time I preached at the Chocolate Bayou Baptist Church, south of Houston. They had asked me to share my death-and-heaven experience.

I was getting my final thoughts together. Typically, in Baptist churches, there is a soloist or some kind of special music just before the guest speaker comes to the pulpit. A woman, who had not been in the service and apparently didn't know what I was going to talk about, came in from a side door to sing. She had a lovely voice and began to sing a song called "Broken and Spilled

Out" about the alabaster jar the woman used when she washed Jesus' feet.

As soon as she sat down, I stood up and began to tell them about my accident. I didn't make any connection between her song and my message, but I noticed that several people kept frowning at the woman.

After the service, I heard someone say to the soloist, "That was an interesting song about being broken and spilled out for you to sing before Don talked." The way he said the word *interesting* really meant *tasteless*.

"Oh!" she said. The shock on her face made me aware that she hadn't known what I was going to speak about. Obviously, she hadn't made the connection either.

Our eyes met and she started to cry. "I'm sorry."

"That's fine," I said. "Really, it's all right." I started to walk on.

"Broken and spilled," someone said. "That's what happened to you, wasn't it?" At least a dozen people made similar comments. A few assumed we had planned for her to sing that particular song.

I stopped and looked back. The soloist stood crying next to the piano. I excused myself and walked back to her. "That's a beautiful song about a wonderful experience. You didn't know what I was going to talk about, but that's all right, because I can't think of a better song."

She started to apologize again.

"It's fine. Really, it's fine," I assured her.

As I walked away, I thought maybe I had been broken and spilled out. But I smiled at another idea: *I'm also being put back together again.*

15 FINDING PURPOSE

Brad Turpin, a motorcycle police officer from the Houston suburb of Pasadena, almost lost a leg. His police motorcycle crashed into the back of a flatbed truck. He would have bled out on the concrete if the EMTs hadn't applied a tourniquet to his leg.

Sonny Steed, the former minister of education at our church, knew Brad personally and asked me to go see him.

"Absolutely," I said, especially after I heard that he would be wearing a fixator. I called and made sure he'd let me come. Before we left, I picked up pictures showing my accident and my recovery.

Sonny drove me to the officer's house. Once we walked inside, it was almost like seeing the way my living room had looked for months. Brad was lying in a hospital bed with the trapeze bar above him. His device was similar, but not quite the same as mine, because in the dozen years since my accident, technology had improved.

Other people were there, so I sat down and joined in casual conversation. He was nice enough, but I knew he'd seen so many people that he was tired of visitors.

As soon as the last visitor left, I said, "You really are tired of talking to people, aren't you?"

Brad nodded.

"I understand. You almost feel like you're on display here. The phone never stops ringing. Everybody wants to come by to see you."

He nodded again. "I appreciate them coming, but I need some peace and quiet."

"I apologize for interrupting you, but Sonny brought me by to see you because I wanted to talk to you about what to expect." I pointed to the Ilizarov and said, "I had one of these external fixators."

"You did?"

I showed him my pictures, beginning with those taken the day after they put on the Ilizarov frame. Each one showed progression to the next step. He stared at each one closely and saw that I had been worse off than he was.

"And you recovered, didn't you?"

"Yes, I did, and so will you."

"That's good that you made it all right, but I don't think I'm going to make it. They can't give me any guarantee that I'm going to keep this leg. The doctors are pessimistic, so that makes it harder for me."

"Well, that's just the way they are," I said, remembering so well my feelings in those early days. "They try not to get your hopes up. They know that months from now, you could have this fixator and everything could be working fine, then your leg could get infected and you could still lose it."

"That's what I mean. I'm just not sure it's worth all this pain."

"The good news is that the pain will ease up as you get better."

His wife had walked in during the conversation and listened. "I'm just so tired at the lack of progress, and nobody will tell us anything," she said. "We're about ready to change doctors."

"You might find a better doctor," I said, "but wait a bit. Be patient. I'm sure your doctor is doing his best."

Then I told them about the time I reached the end of my patience:

"When my doctor came in to see me, I was fuming. 'Sit down,' I yelled. He did, and for maybe five minutes I complained about everything that bothered and upset me. As I watched his face, I realized I had hurt his feelings. I

hadn't been thinking about him, of course. I was hurting, I was never pain free, I couldn't sleep, and I wanted answers. I said, 'I get tired of all this not knowing. I ask you how long I have to wear this, and you say, "Maybe another month, maybe two months, maybe three months."'

"I wasn't through yet, and my anger really burst out with another round of complaints. I ended with, 'Why can't you give me a straight answer?'

"He dropped his head and said softly, 'I'm doing the best I can. I don't know the answers. That's why I can't tell you.'

"'I'm just looking for—'

"'I know you are, but this isn't an exact science. We don't have that much experience in this area, and this is all new technology for us. We're doing the best we can.'"

After I told Brad and his wife about that incident, I added, "Please be patient with your doctor. He can't give you answers he doesn't have. He'll also tell you things to do and load you down with prescriptions. He's going to put you in a lot of therapy, and you're just going to have to learn how to deal with it—all of it."

"Yeah, I know," Brad said, "but I just can't control my emotions anymore. I'm a cop. I've seen a lot of hard, bad, difficult stuff. I find myself just breaking down—I mean, real emotional. Know what I mean?"

"Absolutely. Just go ahead and break down. It'll happen again."

"I feel out of control."

"You are out of control!"

Brad stared at me.

"Think about it. What can you control? Nothing."

"I can't even wipe myself."

"That's right. You're totally helpless. There's nothing you can do or control."

"Before this I was a weight lifter and a bodybuilder," he said. "I had a physique you wouldn't believe."

"I have no doubt about that." I could see that he had once been muscular and strong. "But you don't have that now. You may have a great body again someday, but the inability to get up and do the things that you used to do will cause you to change. Be prepared to change. You're going to lose weight; muscles will atrophy. You can't control your body the way you did before."

His wife was obviously feeling all the stress as well, and she was on the verge of tears. "He feels so bad, even with medication. I just don't know what to do."

"I can suggest a few things. First of all, manage the visits and phone calls. You don't have to let everyone come whenever they want," I said. "Be firm. If you allow everyone to come, you'll wear yourself out trying to be nice. Your friends will understand."

Then I turned to Brad. "Be prepared for all your therapy, because you're going to have to do all kinds of difficult

things. Do them if you want to learn to walk again. Be patient, because it will take a long time."

I paused and almost smiled, because I remembered how I had been. "Let people know where you hurt and how they can help—especially the people you trust. Let them know so they can do things for you. Let them pray for you. You've got a lot of nice folks coming by here, and they want to bring you a cake, cook a meal, or do something for you. Let them express their friendship and love."

After I had talked a few minutes, I got up to leave. I wrote down my phone number. "Call me. If you're struggling to go to sleep at three o'clock in the morning or you're angry, call me. I'll listen. I'll understand because I *can* understand."

Before I left, Brad said, "I can't tell you how much I appreciate your coming by. Just visiting with somebody who knows about the pain helps me a lot. You're the first person I've met who understands what it's like to live with pain twenty-four hours a day."

"It's not something I set out to do—visiting people who are where I was—but I'm willing to do it," I said. "I want to help, but you're going to have to make the effort to call me. Don't try to tough it out alone."

Brad's wife followed me out to the car and said, "He needed this. In public he tries to be the source of strength and sound positive. In quiet moments he's frustrated and emotional, and he falls apart. I've been really worried

about him. Never in our lives together have I seen him this way."

"I remember my wife working hard all day teaching school and then coming to spend the evening with me," I said. "Just hang on with him. He will get better."

I told her that one time when I was at my worst, Eva had tried to encourage me and had said something like, "Just give it time. You're going to be fine."

I had exploded with frustration and rage. "What makes you think I'm going to be fine? What are the odds of my ever being fine? Nobody can ever tell me that. Nobody can promise me that."

To her credit, Eva hadn't argued. She'd wrapped her arms around me. I had wept.

After I told that story to Brad's wife, I said, "Don't take it as a personal attack when he yells or screams. It's the pain and the frustration, not you." I shook her hand and said, "And for goodness' sake, call me if you need me. Push Brad to call me."

After that, I saw Brad four or five times. Weeks later when he was able to get out of the house with his walker, I spotted him in a restaurant. I went over to his table and sat down. "How are you doing?" I asked.

"I'm doing okay. Really okay." He thanked me again for coming at one of his lowest moments. He still wasn't in top shape, but he was getting healthy again. When he clasped my hand and held it a long time, I knew it was

his way of expressing his appreciation in ways he couldn't put into words.

I felt grateful to God for being able to help Brad in his dark time.

✝

About two years after my accident, I heard that Chad Vowell had been in a serious car accident. Chad had been an outstanding soccer player, and he'd been a member of our youth ministry at South Park for about a year before he went to college. His parents were among the most supportive parents I had at the church. His mother, Carol, had been on the committee that came to my hospital room with others to plan youth retreats. I hadn't been very helpful, but it had been their way of making me feel useful and needed.

When I called Carol, I had no idea just how serious Chad was until she said, "He has mangled his lower leg and is in a fixator."

When I heard the word *fixator*, I knew I had to see Chad. I would have gone anyway because he was a member of South Park. But the word *fixator* gave extra urgency.

When I walked into his room, Chad lay there depressed, and he obviously didn't want to talk. This wasn't the Chad I knew. Before that, he'd always been glad to see me, and his face would light up. This time he acknowledged my presence but made no effort to engage in conversation.

"Are you okay? Are you going to be all right?" I asked and then looked at his leg. "I see they gave you a fixator."

"Yeah, they did," he said.

"Chad, you remember when I had my accident? That's the same thing they put on me."

"Really?" he asked. For the first time, he looked at me with interest. I don't know if he'd never seen me with mine or if he just didn't remember. I leaned closer and said, "Just remember this: I know what it feels like to have one of them."

I was able to talk to that young man, hold his hand, and pray with him in a way that made him realize I identified with his plight. For the first time, he had a sense of what he had to look forward to in his treatment. Until then, like me after my accident, no one would give Chad any specific information. Like me, he felt angry and depressed.

"The pain will last a long time, and the recovery will seem to last forever, but you'll get better," I told him. "Just remember that: you will get better."

And he did.

✝

Cancer claimed Joyce Pentecost one week before her thirty-ninth birthday. I had loved her very much. She was married to Eva's brother Eddie and left behind two beautiful redheaded kids, Jordan and Colton.

Not only was Joyce one of the liveliest people I've ever met and a fireball of a singer, but she could also light up a room merely by entering it. She rarely just sang a song; she belted it.

I felt honored to speak at her memorial service. More than six hundred people packed the auditorium. Because Joyce had recorded several CDs of Christian music, she left a legacy for the rest of us. On that sunny afternoon, we heard Joyce sing her own benediction.

Following her recorded music, her father, Reverend Charles Bradley, delivered a message of hope and salvation. He told the crowd, "Years ago Joyce and I made a covenant. If I went first, she would sing at my funeral. And if she went first, I would speak at hers. Today I am fulfilling that promise to my baby girl."

That moment still stays with me. Tears flowed, but I don't think anyone felt anger or hopelessness.

After Joyce's father concluded his message, it was my turn to speak.

"Some may ask today, 'How could Joyce die?'" I said. "But I would say to you the better question is, 'How did she live?' She lived well. She lived very well."

I told the hurting crowd that Joyce was a redheaded comet streaking across the stage of life; that she lived and loved to make people happy; that she was a devoted friend, an ideal daughter, a doting aunt, a sweet sister, a loving mother, and a wonderful wife. I admitted freely that I

didn't have the answer to the question that must have penetrated many hearts in the room: why?

"There is comfort when there are no answers," I said. "Joyce firmly believed that if she died, she would instantly be with God. She believed that if she lived, God would be with her. That was her reason for living. That can be our reason for carrying on."

I concluded by sharing one personal moment. The last conversation I had with Joyce before she returned home from the hospital was about heaven. She never tired of hearing me describe my trip to heaven, so we "visited" there one final time. We talked of the angels, the gate, and our loved ones. Joyce always wanted me to describe the music, and our final conversation together was no different.

"Just a few days ago," I said to the congregation, "I believe God was sitting behind those gates, and he told the angels, 'What we need around here is a good redheaded soprano.'

"'That would be Joyce Pentecost!' the angels said.

"God sent for Joyce, and she answered the call. She is singing now with the angelic hosts. Joyce Pentecost is absent from the body but present with the Lord."

My final words at the service were a question: "Can you lose someone if you know where she is?"

I was thirty-eight years old when I was killed in that car wreck. Joyce was the same age when she was diagnosed

with cancer. I survived the ordeal; Joyce did not. But I know this: because I was able to experience heaven, I was able to prepare her and her loved ones for it. And now I am preparing you.

✝

Many times since my accident I have wished someone who had already gone through the ordeal of wearing a fixator for months had visited me in the hospital. I know it would have relieved a lot of my anxiety.

Whenever I hear about people having a fixator, I try to contact them. When I talk to those facing long-term illness, I try to be totally honest. There is no easy way through that recovery process, and they need to know that. Because I have been there, I can tell them (and they listen) that although it will take a long time, eventually they will get better. I also talk to them about some of the short-term problems they'll face.

My visits with Chad and Brad and others also remind me that God still has a purpose for me on earth. During that long recovery period, I sometimes longed for heaven. Looking back, however, I can see how the personal experiences I have shared with others provided a gentle pull earthward when I was in heaven. "When God is ready to take me," I was finally able to say, "he'll release me." In the meantime, I try to offer as much comfort as possible to others.

Like me, when other victims first see the fixator attached to their leg, and especially when they begin to experience the pain and their inability to move, depression flows through them. They have no idea what's going to happen next. Even though doctors try to reassure them of recovery, they hurt too much to receive comfort from the doctors' words.

Sometimes, however, the patients may be inadvertently misled into saying to me, "I'll get over this soon."

"You may get over it, but it won't be soon," I say. "This is a long-term commitment, and there's no way to speed up the process. There is no easy way out. You have to live with it for now."

I could share other stories, but these are the experiences that kept me going through some of my own dark periods. I found purpose again in being alive. I still long to return to heaven, but for now, this is where I belong. I am serving my purpose here on earth.

16
LONGING FOR HOME

One of my favorite stories is about a little girl who left her house and her mother didn't know where she had gone. Once the mother missed her, she worried that something might have happened to her child. She stood on the front porch and yelled her daughter's name several times.

Almost immediately the little girl ran from the house next door. The mother hugged her, said she was worried, and finally asked, "Where have you been?"

"I went next door to be with Mr. Smith."

"Why were you over there?"

"His wife died, and he is very sad."

"Oh, I'm so sorry, I didn't know that," the mother said. "What did you do?"

"I just helped him cry."

In a way, that's what I do. Sharing my experiences is my way of crying with others in pain.

I've discovered one reason I can bring comfort to people who are facing death themselves or have suffered the loss of a loved one: I've been there.

Without the slightest doubt, I know heaven *is* real. It's more real than anything I've ever experienced in my life. I sometimes say, "Think of the worst thing that's ever happened to you, the best thing that's ever happened to you, and everything in between. Heaven is more real than any of those things."

Since my return to earth, I've been aware that all of us are on a journey. At the end of this life, wherever we go— heaven or hell—life will be more real than this one we're now living. I never thought of that before my accident, of course. Heaven was something I believed in, but I didn't think about it often.

In the years since my accident, I've repeatedly thought of the last night Jesus was with his disciples before his betrayal and crucifixion. Only hours before he began that journey to heaven, he sat with his disciples in the upper room. He begged them not to be troubled and to trust in him. Then he told them he was going away and added, "In my Father's house are many rooms; if it were not so, I

would have told you. I am going there to prepare a place for you. And if I go and prepare a place for you, I will come back and take you to be with me that you also may be where I am" (John 14:2–3).

I had never really noticed it before, but twice Jesus used the word *place*—a location. I think about it often. It is a literal place, and I can testify that I know that place. I've been there. I know heaven is real.

Since my accident, I've felt more deeply than ever before. A year in a hospital bed can do that for anyone, but it was more than just that. Those ninety minutes in heaven left such an impression on me that I can never be the same person I was.

I experienced more pain than I thought a human could endure and still live to tell about it. In spite of all that happened to me during those months of constant pain, I still feel the reality of heaven far, far more than the suffering I endured.

Because I am such a driven person and hardly ever slow down, I have often felt I needed to explain why I can't do certain things. When I'm fully dressed, most folks would never realize I have such injuries. However, when I face an activity that this body just can't do (and people are sometimes surprised how simple some of those acts are), I often get strange responses.

"You look healthy," more than one person has said. "What's the matter with you?"

Occasionally, when I follow someone down a flight of stairs—a difficult experience for me—they hear my knees grinding and turn around. "Is that awful noise coming from you?" they ask.

"Yes." I smile and add, "Isn't it ridiculous!"

I get around better than anyone imagined I would. But I know—even if it doesn't show—that I'm quite limited in what I can do. I work hard to walk properly, because I don't want to attract attention to myself. I had enough stares and gawks when I wore my fixator.

Trying to act and look normal and to keep pushing myself is my way of dealing with my infirmities. I've learned that if I stay busy, especially by helping others, I don't think about my pain. I intend to go on until I can't go anymore.

I believe my greeting committee is still there at the gate. They're waiting. For them, time is not passing. Everything is in the eternal now—although I can't put that into words. Even if ten more years pass, or thirty, in heaven it will be only an instant before I'm back there again.

Going to heaven that January morning wasn't my choice. The only choice in all of this is that one day I had turned to Jesus Christ and accepted him as my Savior. Unworthy as I am, he allowed me to go to heaven, and I know the next time I go there, I'll stay.

I don't have a death wish. I'm not suicidal, but every day I think about going back. I long to return. And I know with utter certainty that I will, in God's timing. Now I

look forward to that time and eagerly await the moment. I have absolutely no fear of death. Why would I? There's nothing to fear—only joy to experience.

As I've pointed out before, when I became conscious again on earth, a bitter disappointment raged through me. I didn't want to return, but it wasn't my choice.

For a long time, I didn't accept that God had sent me back. But even in my disappointment, I knew that God had a purpose in everything that happened. There was a reason I went to heaven and a purpose in my returning. Eventually, I grasped that God had given me a special experience and a glimpse of what eternity will be. Although I long for my heavenly home, I'm prepared to wait until the final summons comes for me.

Going through thirty-four surgeries and many years of pain has also helped me realize the truth of Paul's words to the Corinthians: "Praise be to the God and Father of our Lord Jesus Christ, the Father of compassion and the God of all comfort, who comforts us in all our troubles, so that we can comfort those in any trouble with the comfort we ourselves have received from God" (2 Cor. 1:3–4).

As long as I'm here on earth, God still has a purpose for me. Knowing that fact enables me to endure the pain and cope with my physical disabilities. In my darkest moments, I remember a line from an old song: "It will be worth it all when we see Jesus."

I know it will.

17
THE WHY QUESTIONS

One time I shared my experiences with a large congregation that included my wife's parents, Eldon and Ethel Pentecost. They've been consistently supportive and made great sacrifices during my accident and lengthy recovery.

After the service, we went to their home. At one point, Eldon and I were alone, and he told me, "I was angry the first time you shared your story of your trip to heaven."

I had no idea he felt that way.

"You finished by saying you never wanted to come back to earth."

I just nodded, not knowing where this was going.

"I didn't understand it then, but I've changed. Now when I hear you talk about heaven's beauty, I understand a little better why you'd willingly be separated from my daughter and grandkids for a while. You know—you really do know, don't you—that they'll join you someday?"

"Without a doubt," I said.

Eldon's comment had caught me off guard. He was right, of course. I had the distinct privilege of baptizing

my own children and seeing my wife baptized as well. By faith, I knew that they would be residents of heaven someday. Being separated from them had never crossed my mind while I was in heaven. People in heaven simply don't have an awareness of who is *not* there. They do know who is coming.

Even today, I can say honestly that I wish I could have stayed in heaven, but my ultimate time had not yet come. After leaving heaven, if I had known that I would face two weeks in ICU, a year in a hospital bed, and thirty-four operations, I surely would have been even more disheartened.

However, leaving heaven was not my choice, and I returned to the sounds of one voice praying, boots crunching glass underfoot, and the Jaws of Life ripping through my shattered auto.

✝

One question keeps troubling me: *why?* It takes many forms.

Why did I die in that car wreck?

Why did I have the unique privilege of going to heaven?

Why did I glimpse heaven, only to be sent back?

Why did I nearly die in the hospital?

Why has God let me live in constant pain since January 18, 1989?

The short answer: I don't know. By nature, we're curious. We want to know.

I still don't know why such things happen. I do know God is with me in the darkest moments of life.

Besides asking why, there are other questions. I think they're even more important for me to ponder.

Did God want me to know how real pain could feel so that I could understand the pain of others?

Did God want me to know how real heaven is?

What did God want me to learn from all my experiences, my death, and the long period of recovery?

How can my experiences be of benefit to others?

After all these years, I don't have the answers to most of those questions either. I have learned a few things and realize that God still has reasons for keeping me alive on earth. But even though I don't have full answers to my questions, I do have peace. I know I am where God wants me to be. I know I'm doing the work God has given me.

I find comfort in a story recorded in John's Gospel. A man born blind meets Jesus and is healed. After that, he runs around praising God, but his healing is an embarrassment to the religious leaders who have been trying to turn the people against Jesus. They try to force the man to admit that Jesus is a sinner (that is, a fraud). The man wisely says, "Whether he is a sinner or not, I don't know. One thing I do know. I was blind but now I see!" (John 9:25).

In the same way, some may not believe my account, but I don't have to defend my experience. I know what happened to me. For those of us whose faith is in the reality of heaven, no amount of evidence is necessary. *I know what I experienced.*

I believe God gave me a hint of what eternity in heaven will be like.

I also believe that part of the reason I am still alive, as I've already pointed out, is that people prayed. Dick Onerecker prayed me back to life—to live without brain damage. David Gentiles and others prayed so that God wouldn't take me back to heaven just yet.

I am here, I am alive, and it's because God's purposes have not yet been fulfilled in my life. When God is finished with me, I'll return to the place I yearn to be. I have made my final reservations for heaven, and I'm going back someday—permanently.

Prayerfully, I'll see you there too.

Don Piper has been an ordained minister since 1985 and has served in several capacities on church staffs, including six years as a senior pastor. He also was a pastor for children for three years. He and his wife, Eva, are residents of Pasadena, Texas, and are the parents of three grown children and one grandchild. Don has appeared on many television and radio programs and has been the subject of countless newspaper and magazine features. He used to write a weekly newspaper column, and every week you will find him preaching and leading conferences and retreats all over the United States and abroad. Don has written three other books about answered prayer, finding a better life today, and having an eternal life someday. Don can be contacted at donpiperministries@yahoo.com.

Cecil Murphey has written or coauthored more than one hundred books, including his work on the autobiography of Franklin Graham, *Rebel with a Cause*. Cecil can be contacted at www.cecilmurphey.com.

The Book That Started It All . . .

A true story of *death* and *life*

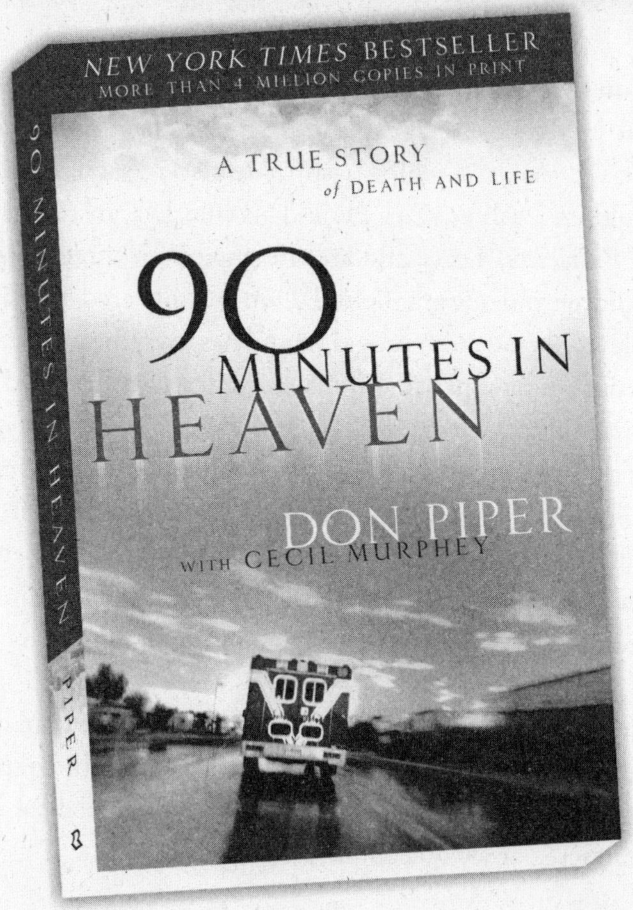